Praise for
The Cycle of the Gift

"From abundance to 'affluenza'—how often families unwittingly create what they most dread! A generous spirit and crystal-clear values are the foundation that protect a family from spiraling into dysfunction and entitlement. *The Cycle of the Gift* is the perfect blueprint for those who wish their giving to be a true gift."

—*Charlotte B. Beyer, Founder & Former CEO, Institute for Private Investors, Investor Education Collaborative*

"This is a remarkable book. It truly helps illuminate the issues and breakthrough conversations that families can have around giving to their children and grandchildren."

—*Charles W. Collier, Former Senior Philanthropic Advisor, Harvard University*

"The authors have given the reader much to consider—the spirit of giving, the desired effect when making gifts, and the function of the gift over the form. Like *Family Wealth*, this book puts a spotlight on the most important questions for family members to contemplate when making gifts and offers the potential for completely different outcomes from the experience. If you read this book, you will not have to ask, 'how much is enough?'"

—*Sara Hamilton, Founder and CEO, Family Office Exchange*

"With thoughtfulness and clarity based on a multi-discipline collaboration of considerable expertise, Jay Hughes, Susan Massenzio and Keith Whitaker challenge readers to mindfully consider the dynamics which occur between a gift giver and the recipient. *The Cycle of the Gift* is an invaluable resource for both individuals and the advisory community so that the 'spirit of the gift' is one that will enable the receiver to integrate it in a manner which will contribute to self-actualization and flourishing."

—*Dr. Lee Hausner, Managing Director,*
First Foundation Advisors

"*The Cycle of the Gift: Family Wealth and Wisdom* is a must read for affluent families. It deals with one of the most difficult and profound issues: how much should I give and what process should I follow? It provides powerful insights to help family members become mindful givers and receivers. The authors do a remarkable job of spotlighting the spiritual benefits a family can enjoy through giving. As the book so eloquently details, it is one thing to give but an entirely different activity to ensure the gift will have a positive impact on those who will benefit."

—*Mel Lagomasino, CEO, GenSpring Family Offices*

"This extraordinary book is a gift. Its contribution is helping us understand the complete cycle of any gift. I was particularly touched by the dynamics between the giver and recipient, and how emotional and misunderstood it can be. The true gift of this book and of its writers is turning awkward situations and even pain … into joy!"

—*Thomas R. Livergood, CEO, The Family Wealth Alliance*

"The best learning comes when a book is able to take something that you do and consider important, and guide you to step back and look with fresh eyes to see how you are wasting opportunities and possibilities that are easily adopted. *The Cycle of the Gift* takes the process of giving, a foundation of all society, and takes us on a journey to understand its deeper nature. The core idea—that the act of delivering the gift is not complete in itself, but rather one that depends on deeper reflection on its intention, context, and communication to fulfill its purpose. The book is philosophical, taking us deeper, but also practical, with stories and clear actions, that will truly transform your relations with the people you care about."

—*Dennis Jaffe, Saybrook University*

"These well-versed authors offer a golden blend of technically astute practical guidance and the foundational spiritual and classical knowledge of wisdom, discernment, and counsel."

—*Paul G. Schervish, Professor and Director of the Center on Wealth and Philanthropy at Boston College*

"Families with wealth face a great and persistent challenge: how to give to children and grandchildren in ways that enhance their lives rather than creates dependency. *The Cycle of the Gift* faces this challenge squarely with sound and prudent counsel. If leaving a legacy is important to you, this is a must read."

—*James P. Steiner, President, Abbot Downing, a Wells Fargo Business*

The Cycle
of the Gift

Since 1996, Bloomberg Press has published books for financial professionals, as well as books of general interest in investing, economics, current affairs, and policy affecting investors and business people. Titles are written by well-known practitioners, BLOOMBERG NEWS® reporters and columnists, and other leading authorities and journalists. Bloomberg Press books have been translated into more than 20 languages.

For a list of available titles, please visit our Web site at www .wiley.com/go/bloombergpress.

The Cycle of the Gift

Family Wealth and Wisdom

James E. Hughes
Susan E. Massenzio
Keith Whitaker

BLOOMBERG PRESS
An Imprint of
WILEY

Cover Design: Wendy Mount
Cover Image: © Mondadori Portfolio/UIG/Getty Images

Copyright © 2013 by James E. Hughes, Susan E. Massenzio, and Keith Whitaker.

Published by John Wiley & Sons, Inc., Hoboken, New Jersey.
Published simultaneously in Canada.

For general information on our other products and services or for technical support, please contact our Customer Care Department within the United States at (800) 762-2974, outside the United States at (317) 572-3993 or fax (317) 572-4002.

Wiley publishes in a variety of print and electronic formats and by print-on-demand. Some material included with standard print versions of this book may not be included in e-books or in print-on-demand. If this book refers to media such as a CD or DVD that is not included in the version you purchased, you may download this material at http://booksupport.wiley.com. For more information about Wiley products, visit www.wiley.com.

Library of Congress Cataloging-in-Publication Data:

Hughes, James E., Jr.
     The cycle of the gift [electronic resource] : family wealth and wisdom / James E. Hughes, Susan E. Massenzio, Keith Whitaker.
          1 online resource.
          Includes index.
     Description based on print version record and CIP data provided by publisher; resource not viewed.
       ISBN 978-1-118-48759-4 (cloth); ISBN 978-1-118-48837-9 (ebk) ;
       ISBN 978-1-118-48834-8 (ebk) ; ISBN 978-1-118-48836-2 (ebk)
          1. Families.   2. Wealth.   3. Families—Economic aspects.   4. Estate planning.
     I. Massenzio, Susan E.   II. Whitaker, Albert Keith.   III. Title.
     HQ734
     306.85— dc23

                                                                              2012033837

Printed in the United States of America
10 9 8

To Peter Karoff, whose gift to me of his question "what about a family's spiritual capital" inspired this book, thank you

To Jacqueline Merrill, who put her arm through mine, thank you.

—Jay Hughes

To my mother, whose spirit of giving and receiving well I have internalized. Thank you.

To my wonderful son, who teaches me how to give and receive wisely. Thank you. May you continue to flourish.

To Nancy Lundy and my dear friends: I treasure your gifts of friendship. Thank you.

To my family: thank you for being there.

—Susan Massenzio

To my family,
  To my friends,
  And to my loving partner, who is the greatest gift of all.

—Keith Whitaker

To Anne D'Andrea, the fourth author of this book: without your contributions to our collaboration this book would never have been born. Thank you.

—From all of us

The person who kindly guides another on his way,
Lights as it were another's lantern from his own
Nor is his light the less for kindling the other.

—Cicero, *On Duties*

Contents

Preface   xv
Acknowledgments   xix
Introduction   xxv

Chapter 1   The Elephant in the Room   **1**
              Grandparents' Checks   2
              When Giving Becomes an Opportunity   4

Chapter 2   The Spirit of the Gift   **7**
              Where the Spirit Leads   11

                   The Who of Giving

Chapter 3   Becoming a Wise Giver   **17**
              Know Thyself   18
              How Much?   21
              Guilt and Remorse   24
              Nothing Too Much   26

Chapter 4   **Receiving Wisely**   **29**
             A Bad Investment?   30
             The Psychological Stages of Giving   32
             Giving and the Work Ethic   36
             Not Yet   39
             Meteors and Resilience   41
             Investing in Recipients   44

Chapter 5   **Spouses**   **47**
             Learning from Yourselves and Each Other   47
             Three-Step Process   48
             Blended Families   50
             Prenuptial Discussions   51
             Fiscal Unequals   54

Chapter 6   **Grandparents**   **57**
             Grandparents' Great Opportunity   57
             Involving Parents   58
             Grandparents and Philanthropy   61

Chapter 7   **Trustees**   67
             The Choice of Trustee   67
             The Type of Trustee   69
             The Relationship between Beneficiary
             and Trustee   69
             A Regenerative Role   74

Chapter 8   **Elders**   77
             Intergenerational Dynamics   78
             Growing Elders   79
             The Work of Elders   81

                       The How of Giving

Chapter 9   **Control versus Freedom**   **87**
             The Myth of the Free Gift   87
             Cui Bono?   88

	The Giving of Accounts	90
	Letting Be	92
Chapter 10	**Fair versus Equal, Separate versus Together**	**97**
	The Balancing Act	98
	Pot Shots	100
	Flourishing	102
	Promises	103
Chapter 11	**Giving Outright, via Loans, or in Trust?**	**107**
	Options	108
	Sharing the Spirit	108
	Making Loans Work	109
	Why Trusts?	110
	The Family Bank	113
	Form versus Function	115

The What and Why of Giving

Chapter 12	**What Families Give**	**121**
	Homes	121
	Business Interests	125
	Values	131
	Rituals	134
	Reputation	136
Chapter 13	**The Why of Giving**	**141**
	Why *Not*	142
	The Family Tree	144
	Giving Thanks	146
About the Authors		151
Index		155

Preface

The Cycle of the Gift: Family Wealth and Wisdom invites you on a journey into the subject of giving within families. Before setting off, we want to offer a word about our own journey into this topic.

Every book has its precedents, and in this case the most important is our co-author Jay Hughes's book Family Wealth: Keeping It in the Family. Writing that book brought Jay face-to-face with a question that he posed but did not answer: "Can a family succeed over the long term without a spiritual component at its core?"[1] The Cycle of the Gift reflects on this question and is meant to fill the gap that Family Wealth acknowledged.

Many families' estate plans focus on tax minimization: an understandable but often unreflective goal. Few are truly mindful, meaning conscious, of the emotional effects on recipients as well as of the true intentions of the person doing the planning. This book encourages mindfulness about ourselves and our families. It offers giving as a way into the spiritual core of individual and family flourishing: something we call the "spirit of the gift."

Family Wealth was a precursor to this book in another, very practical way. Its publication brought the three of us together to address a particular concern: how to help families ensure that their material resources have positive effects on their individual members, their families, their communities, and the world.

For each of us, the journey to that point started with the experience of lineage, a term about which we'll have more to say later on. For Jay, that lineage came in the form of his being a sixth-generation attorney-at-law and a recipient of the wisdom of his father. Susan received the lineage embodied in the profession of psychology and the gifts of resilience, optimism, and possibility she received from her mother and grandmother. For Keith, the journey began with the gift of the heritage of classical antiquity, which he received from his high school Latin teacher, and the gift of the examples of scholarship and public engagement given to him by both his parents. Though beneficiaries of different lineages, all three of us sought to turn these gifts to the question of how to help people flourish.

The path of writing this book has had many twists and turns. As many families do, we began by putting most of our thinking into the question, How can I give well? But in practice, much of the difficulty people face is in *receiving* well. Giving due attention to *recipients* was a breakthrough for us. Everyone loves a giver. But how many of us love recipients—or love to be a recipient? The difficulties faced by recipients brought us eventually to see the role of spirit in giving. And that recognition connected our current work with the question that Jay had raised but left unanswered in *Family Wealth*. In a wonderful way, our writing has completed a cycle of its own.[2]

Our journey has been one of going deep into a particular subject—giving within families—a study that led eventually to a realm that transcends that subject. The spirit of the gift is in some ways a simple matter; indeed, it had been there in front of us all that time. Yet it took a "beginner's mind" to see it.[3] We invite you now to join us in the journey. Our hope is that these pages will help your family and you approach this simple but profound topic with the mindfulness that embodies "the spirit of the gift."

Notes

Visit our website at www.thecycleofthegift.com for a regularly updated bibliography of readings related to giving and family wealth.

1. See James E. Hughes, *Family Wealth: Keeping It in the Family* (Princeton, NJ: NetWrx, Inc., 1997), v–vi, or James E. Hughes, *Family Wealth: Keeping It in the Family* (New York: Bloomberg Press, 2004), xv–xvi. Further references will be to the latter, revised edition.

2. If it seems odd that a later work should be the prequel to an earlier one, we recall what Aristotle often said: "What is first for us is not necessarily first by nature."

3. "For the way to what is near is always the longest and thus the hardest for us humans. This way is the way of meditative thinking." Martin Heidegger, *Discourse on Thinking*, trans. John M. Anderson and E. Hans Freund (New York: Harper Torchbooks, 1966), 55.

Acknowledgments

Foster Aborn
Richard and Carey Ach
Stacey Allred
Thad Alston
David and Sharmie Altshuler
Patricia Angus
Chris and Judy Armstrong
Kristen Armstrong
Pat Armstrong
Richard Bakal
Steven Barimo
Edward Bastian
Frank Baylin
David Beatty
Timothy J. Belber
Rhett Bennett
Melissa Berman
Linda Betts

Charlotte Beyer
Darcy Bhatia
Geoffrey and Jane Biddle
Art Black
Bill Boer
Drew Bottaro
Arne Boudewyn
Daniel and Susan Boyce
Susan Bradley
Joanie Bronfman
Fredda Herz Brown
Tim Brown
Jean and Debbie Brunel
G. Scott Budge, PhD
Ulrich Burkhard
Natalie and Matt Burton
Paul Cameron
Randy Carlock

Marty Carter
Diana Chambers
Michelle Clements
Gail E. Cohen
David Cohn
Michael Cole
Charles Collier
Paul Comstock
Jay Cowles
Matt Crawford
Merial Currier
Greg Curtis
Kim Curtis
Darlene Dahl-Legro
Anne D'Andrea
John Davis
Peter Davis
Francois DeVissher
Joan DiFuria
Richard Dinsmore
Ann Dugan
Mary Duke
John P. C. Duncan
Bryan Dunn
Stephen Eide
Ed Eskandarien
Ginny Esposito
Peter Evans
Paul Ferguson
Kate Fering
Joseph A. Field
Betsy and Jesse Fink
Michael Fisher
Richard E. Fogg

Robert Frank
Doug Freeman
David Friedman
Priscilla Friesen
Jon and Eileen Gallo
Dan and Barbara Garvey
Tony Gary
Kelin Gersick
Lisa Kirby Gibbs
Barbara and Robert Gibson
Holly Gibson
Jack Ginter
Joline Godfrey
Stephen Goldbart
Sharna Goldseker
Hartley Goldstone
Davidson T. Gordon
Robert Gordon
James Grubman
Tony and Eve Guernsey
Jamie Gutteridge
Sara Hamilton
Anne Hargrave
George N. and Karen Harris
Bonnie Hartley
Mike Hartley
Lloyd Hascoe
Barbara Hauser
Lee Hausner
Eric Hayes
Alan F. Heath
Katherine Heath
Jane Hilbert-Davis
Robert H. N. Ho

Robert Y. C. Ho
Steven Hoch
Mike Hogan
David Horn
Jack J. T. Huang
James and Elizabeth Hughes
Peter and Agneta Hughes
William and Alyssa Johl Hughes
Neen Hunt
Mary Elizabeth Hutton
Adrienne Iglehart
Dennis Jaffe
Mark Jenness
Jim Jones
Bruce Judelson
Dirk Junge
Wendy Kane
Amy and Leon Kass
Rob Kaufold
Kristen Keffeler
Eric Kessler
Daniel Kinder
Katie Kinsey
Nancy-Elizabeth and
 Christopher Knowdell
Donald D. and Adele Kozusko
William Krisel
Kaycee Krysty
Irwin Kula
Yumi and Eiichiro Kuwana
Maria Elena Lagomasino
Ivan Lansberg
Jim and Susan Lawson
Peter Leach

Gene Lipitz
Deborah Lockwood
Susan and Fred Lodge
Charles Lowenhaupt
Bill Lyons
Kim Schneider Malek
James Mann
Barnaby Marsh
Steve Martiros
Marilyn Mason
Valerie Maxwell
Kathryn McCarthy
Ross McClellan
George McCully
King McGlaughon
Mary Ann McGuigan
Paul McKibbon
Jamie McLaughlin
Rui Mendes
Drew S. Mendoza
Steven Merrill
Bill Messinger
Juan and Virginia Meyer
Leon M. and Joan Meyers
Ed and Janet Miller
Lee Miller
Isabel Miranda
Gay Mitchell
Curt and Sara Moll
Jan Moll
Robert Moser
Susan Mucciarone
Brad Nystedt
Bill O'Brien

John and Patricia O'Neil

Steve Oliver

Ed Orazem

Dave Osborne

Clyde Ostler

Randall Ottinger

Karen Owensby

Gerri Pangaro

Richard Pease

Judith Stern Peck

Jennifer Pendergast

Scott R. Peppet

Ellen Perry and Rob Stein

Henry and Cecilia Perry

Caroline Pfohl

Kenneth Polk

Victor Preisser

Dan Prickett

Courtney Pullen

Abby Raphael

Reginald Ray

Ellen Remmer

John Rhodes

Gregory T. Rogers

Tom Rogerson

Ned and Catherine Rollhaus

Kirby Rosplock

Laurent Roux

Myra Salzer

Suresh Sani

William Schambra

Paul Schervish

Desmond Shum and Whitney
  Duan

Gary Shunk

John Simmering

Louise Smith

Michael J. A. Smith

Hill C. Snellings

Steve and Jamie Snyder

Peter Steinglass

Howard Stephenson

Christian Stewart

Molly Stranahan

Bente Strong

Betsy and Rob Templeton

Tamara Termohlen

Heath Thomson

Nick Thomson

Jamie Trager-Muney

John J. Trask

David C. Trott

Jonathan D. Trott

Ken and Debra Tuchman

Maarten Van Hengel

Steve Vetter

Rhonda E. Vogel

Michael Vogelzang

Tim Volk

Barry Waldorf

John Ward

Rashad Wareh

John and Carol Warnick

Chester Weber

Ellen and John Webster

Philippe Weil

Peter A. White

Rick and Rebecca White

Stephen Wilchins
Roy Williams
John Williamson
Thayer Willis
Hunter Wilson
Scott Winget
Kathy Wiseman
Rosalie Wolf

Peter Wood
Vincent Worms
Ralph and Toni Wyman
Kana Yamada
Danielle Oristian York
Amy Zehnder
Cummings Zuill

Introduction

As we will see, the spirit of the gift moves our attention away from gifts as things and toward the people involved in giving: who they are as well as what they do. As a result, after two introductory chapters, we have divided this book into three main parts. First, "The Who of Giving" deals with the people most deeply involved in family giving, especially givers and recipients. Second, "The How of Giving" takes up several ways that giving can enhance family life. And third, "The What and Why of Giving" describes various types of gifts, from homes to business interests to values and rituals. This part also addresses the key question of whether it is in fact wise to give to family members at all.

The chapters within each of these three parts build on each other but not in lockstep. Each offers something of its own. Each one also ends with a question for your personal reflection and discussion with family members, friends, or trusted advisors. For a regularly updated bibliography of readings on giving and family wealth, please visit www.thecycleofthegift.com.

What follows is a brief summary of the themes addressed in the respective chapters.

Giving wisely. The first step toward wisdom is to clear your lenses. Parents often ask us, "How much is enough to leave my children?" Before addressing that question, ask yourself, how much is enough for me? To move from the quantitative to a qualitative focus, we offer readers two classical precepts: *know thyself* and *nothing too much.*

Receiving wisely. Receiving well is the only way to sustain the spirit and cycle of the gift. Preparing wise recipients requires understanding each recipient, adult or child. Who is he or she? It involves helping recipients find the meaning of work and the resilience to adapt to and integrate the meteoric effects of a significant gift.

Spouses. Family giving often involves giving with a spouse or partner. It is crucial to clarify your own and your spouse's dreams and wishes and to communicate about gifts. This is especially so for couples with blended families or inequalities of wealth.

Grandparents. Grandparents have their own special considerations as givers. Grandparents and grandchildren do not face as great a challenge in separating from each other as parents and children do. As a result, grandparents can often give more freely. But giving well requires thoughtful communication with adult children and new ways to interact with grandchildren, such as through philanthropy.

Trustees. Instead of being merely administrators or investors, trustees can help beneficiaries mature and thereby use the trust-gift to enhance, rather than merely to subsidize, beneficiaries' lives. They can also model the cycle of the gift for each generation, regenerating its power.

Elders. Elders are people who have done their work and are ready to focus on their good and the good of the family as a whole. They embody the activity of discernment, namely, the ability to connect a vision of the human good with the particular choices we have before us here and now.[1]

Control versus freedom. We begin our discussion of the *how* of giving with a core consideration: Givers often want to exert some control while making gifts freely. Likewise, recipients often want to remain connected with the giver while being free to use the gift as they wish. We offer ways to separate out these elements of control. True gifts promote the freedom of both givers and recipients.

Fair versus equal. Parents want to do what is best for each child, but they also want to treat their children equally. This is one of the greatest challenges to giving. We offer thoughts on managing this challenge well with honest self-reflection and communication.

Outright gifts, loans, and trusts. Outright gifts are the simplest transactions but difficult to infuse with spirit. Loans can leverage gifts but require lots of communication if they are not to undermine beneficiaries' habits regarding credit. Trusts are extremely useful but also challenging. We offer the family bank as a model that combines loans, trusts, and outright gifts with spirit. It embodies a set of practices aimed at family growth above all.

Homes. We begin discussing the *what* of giving with one of the most common family gifts: the family's primary or vacation home. Such a gift exerts great power because it strongly embodies spirit. It takes honest conversations to give it well.

Business interests. Families with businesses must bring special consideration and even more careful communication to their gifts. In particular, they do well to ensure that ownership and management of the company do not overshadow membership in the family.

Values and giving. Most people say that they want to give their children their values above all. We take up such questions as, how can parents make such an intangible gift effectively? And how can they help their children receive their values rather than feel imposed upon?

Rituals. Whenever it occurs, giving generates that special combination of playfulness and solemnity known as ritual. We explore why rituals matter to families and how they can function as gifts.

Reputation. If you are part of a family, you participate in the family's reputation, often embodied in the family name. But reputation is much more than public image; it is lineage, a very special type of gift. We explore lineage and stories as critical gifts.

Why we give. To conclude, we turn to the question, *why* give to family? We consider many people's serious concerns regarding family gifts and inheritances. We then explain that the thinking and activities we have shared show how family giving can foster human excellence—and even display it. We single out two forms of excellence central to family giving: humility and giving thanks. And we reflect on the power of the spirit of the gift to enhance the whole of life, within and beyond our families.

Some Key Terms and Images

A number of terms and images appear throughout this book, like threads through a tapestry. We want to highlight a few of the most important ones here, so that you can keep them in mind while reading. Our hope is that they gain in meaning and depth as you read the following pages and reflect on their application to your life.

The spirit of the gift is our most important term. As we will discuss in Chapter 2, *spirit* combines the giver's intentions with the gift's own qualities. Even more, a gift with spirit causes both the giver and the recipient to grow and to feel free. And it spurs recipients to give in turn, perpetuating the cycle of the gift. A gift without spirit we call a *transfer*.

A central image for us is that of the gift as *meteor* (See Figure I.1). It flies from the giver to the recipient, often appearing on the

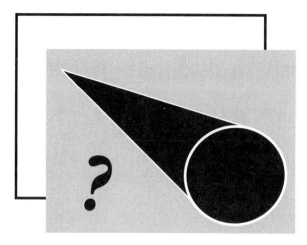

Figure I.1   Meteoric Gifts

recipient's horizon with no warning. Its impact can upend the recipient's environment. As a result, we ask, how can you help recipients prepare to receive this meteor well? And perhaps most importantly, what's in your meteor?

Recipients, however, are not passive satellites. Ultimately, our hope is that recipients learn to *adapt to* and *integrate* the gift-meteor. This is no small matter. The result of that adaptation and integration—or lack thereof—will decisively affect a recipient's life. We use these equations to sum up its importance:

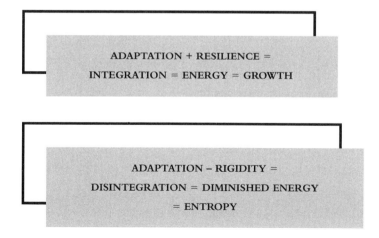

ADAPTATION + RESILIENCE =
INTEGRATION = ENERGY = GROWTH

ADAPTATION – RIGIDITY =
DISINTEGRATION = DIMINISHED ENERGY
= ENTROPY

Discussions of wealth almost always focus on *quantity*. One of our main goals in this book is to redirect that focus to *quality*. The difference is crucial: It is the difference between how much you have versus how well you live.

Closely connected are the terms *subsidy* and *enhancement*. A subsidy adds quantitatively but not qualitatively to life. It gives you more of what you have, but by doing so it may siphon off your energy and aspirations. An enhancement promotes growth. It may not make you richer, but it does make you more able. Continued long enough, subsidies cement *entitlement*. Enhancements lay the ground for true *freedom*.

Besides focusing on quantity, discussions of wealth or giving also usually focus on *form*: that is, on the structures or entities that will hold the wealth. But this attention to form too often ignores these structures' *function*. If you want to promote growth and freedom, form must serve function. Otherwise, functionless forms will sap individuals' and the family's energy.

Much of family giving takes place within the context of estate planning, and such planning, in our view, can be unreflective, thoughtful, or mindful. *Unreflective* giving is not bad, but it follows the unquestioned assumption that more is better: Squeeze the most quantity into the cleverest forms to maximize tax savings. *Thoughtful* givers take a step further: Instead of just accepting the experts' assumption that more is better, they ask, what is the right thing to do? What gifts or ways of giving align with my values?

Our goal is to take one more step and to promote mindful giving. *Mindful* giving includes understanding yourself as a giver, understanding the recipient of your gift, and understanding that the quality of your relationship will directly affect your ability to give well, the recipient's ability to receive well, and your respective abilities to feel freer as a result of the gift.

These stages of giving bring us to one last image: that of a *helping hand*. It comes to us from the great medieval Jewish philosopher Maimonides, who famously describes eight levels of giving, somewhat like rungs on a ladder.[2] At the bottom of this ladder is grudging or reluctant giving. In the middle are more or less dutiful forms of giving. Second highest is completely anonymous giving, in which the giver does not know who received his gift and the recipient does not know who gave it. These completely anonymous gifts free the giver and recipient from complicated feelings of control, guilt, or resentment.

But the highest level of all, Maimonides says, "is where one takes the other's hand and gives him a gift or loan, or makes a partnership with him, or finds him employment, in order to strengthen him until he needs to ask help of no one." This wonderful image breaks down the inequalities of wealth and power so often present in giving. It promises the possibility of freedom and equality, for both giver and recipient. It also promises a sense of true togetherness: hand in hand, face-to-face. No doubt it is rare and not always possible. But our hope is that, through mindfulness, our giving can embody the spirit of the helping hand.

Notes

1. For more on discernment (mainly within the context of philanthropic giving), see Paul Schervish and Keith Whitaker, *Wealth and the Will of God* (Bloomington: Indiana University Press, 2010). See also Chapter 4.

2. Maimonides describes these levels in his *Mishneh Torah*, in the section on "Laws Concerning Gifts to the Poor." For a translation of and introduction to the eight levels, see Amy A. Kass, ed., *Giving Well, Doing Good* (Bloomington: Indiana University Press, 2008), 95–96. We have based our translation on Kass's.

Chapter 1

The Elephant in the Room

Giving within families is a phenomenon that most people hesitate to talk about. Even in the midst of recessions and crises, tens of thousands of households across the globe have the wherewithal to make regular gifts of cash or securities to their children and grandchildren. And practically all parents, no matter how slender their means, dream of leaving something to their children after death. For anyone with parents, children, or grandchildren, giving to "your own" occupies a key place in life.

So why do we not discuss it more? Why is it not as much a part of public discussion as giving to nonfamily members, in the form of philanthropy or charity? More to the point, why is it so hard to discuss such giving where it really counts—in the confines of our own homes and in the bosom of our families? Perhaps a brief story will begin to answer these questions.

Grandparents' Checks

We met a couple we'll call Adele and Albert when they were in their early 80s. He had been a senior executive at a Fortune 500 company. They have several adult children, a host of grandchildren, and even a few great-grandchildren. Albert's career, which Adele dutifully supported, had earned them tens of millions of dollars.

As a result, they had what is called in the financial world an estate tax problem. If they were to die, their estate would be subject to significant taxes—at a rate of at least 50 percent—before passing to their heirs. Adele and Albert are philanthropic and give each year to several charities, and they know that these gifts help reduce their taxable estate. But their main desire is to pass their values and their hard-earned wealth to their descendants.

On the advice of their accountant, Adele and Albert had for many years made what are known as *annual exclusion gifts* (so called because the amounts given are excluded from consideration for gift tax), first to their children and then eventually to their grandchildren and great-grandchildren. They also included their children's spouses. By making such gifts, they have been able to move tens of thousands of dollars each year out of their estate to their descendants, tax free.

Taking from Giving

Yes, the United States government, and many other governments, tax even gifts, at least those over a certain amount (currently $13,000). Congress instituted the gift tax in 1932, 16 years after the estate tax, to keep parents from avoiding the estate tax by giving all their assets to their children right before death. In 1976, Congress also created the generation-skipping tax to capture gifts that skip a generation and benefit grandchildren or further descendants. These three taxes—the estate tax, the gift tax, and the generation-skipping tax—are together known as transfer taxes.

So every December Adele and Albert would sit down with the checkbook and a list of family members' names, write the checks, and give them to the accountant, and he would send them off to their recipients. Then the couple noticed something: These gifts were vanishing without an echo. Few or no thank you notes arrived. No thank-you calls.

This silence got them wondering. Were their family members receiving the gifts? Yes. Were they ungrateful? Adele and Albert hoped not. Sure, their family is not perfect: They do not get along with one of their sons, with whom they speak only rarely. Another son went through a bitter divorce, and as a result they do not see his children more than once a year. A couple of grandchildren suffer from addictions and so their gifts go into trusts that they cannot access freely. But even with these issues, Adele and Albert found their family members to be generally decent people who know how to say thank you.

The lack of response began to make them wonder about the money's effects. Had their children and grandchildren simply gotten used to the annual gifts? Were they treating those checks more like everyday income rather than something extra? Had the checks become mere subsidies, taken for granted rather than enhancing their children's and grandchildren's lives? Even worse, had these subsidies created dependency and entitlement, which the children and grandchildren were reluctant to reveal? Adele was a mischievous lady and so she asked Albert, "What if this year we just 'forgot' to send the checks?"

Albert reflected on Adele's question and decided to take the matter up in a thoughtful manner consistent with his character. This is the point at which they involved us. We had the opportunity to speak with the children, their spouses, and many of the grandchildren. As predicted, they turned out to be generally good people—not perfect but more often than not trying to do the right thing.

We brought up with them the annual exclusion gifts, and they responded with as many questions as we had from Adele and Albert. One of the children's spouses, for example, had grown up in a blue-collar family. Once she was married—without a word of preparation—$20,000 checks from her parents-in-law started showing up in her mailbox each December, as she put it, "like a meteor!" She had never received more than a few hundred dollars as a gift before. She did not know what the right thing was to do in response.

Adele and Albert's estranged son suspected his parents of trying to buy his affection. He blamed them for not sending a card or note with the check. He feared that "Mom and Dad's money" came with strings attached. Also, he was angry with his parents for giving money to his three children (their grandchildren) without his input or oversight as their father. He worried that his parents' generosity would create dependency and entitlement in his own children. (He did not know that his parents were worried about the very same thing with respect to him!) His reaction reflected the levels of hurt that existed between him and his parents that eclipsed the money.

One of Adele and Albert's daughters summed up her response to her parents' checks very simply. She knew from reading books on finance that such gifts were a regular part of estate planning. She was grateful to receive the money, but she also wondered, "Are these really gifts for *me*? Or are they just a tax-reduction tactic for Mom and Dad?"

Why had she or her siblings not asked Adele and Albert some of these questions? They all had more or less the same response: "It's their business and their money. I would not want to pry. I would appear ungrateful!"

When Giving Becomes an Opportunity

Adele and Albert's story reveals some of the reasons that most families have trouble discussing gifts or hide them behind a veil of silence. Even when not involving millions of dollars, family giving raises questions of control, expectations, caring, respect and responsibility, privacy and publicity, and freedom and dependence, not to mention favor and fairness. Given the tension such questions can generate, it is no surprise that many families decide to act first and talk later—or not at all.

But where there are questions, there are also opportunities. Family life does involve control, love, justice, and fairness. That is just another way of saying that it introduces us to some of the most serious aspects of life in general. And it requires that we come to terms with those matters again and again. We have choices, not just in what we give or to whom we give, but also in how we give, how we receive, and how we talk about these things. In making those choices, we have opportunities to give and receive well.

What does *well* mean? For family giving, *well* takes its meaning from the well-being of family, which we capture with the term *family flourishing*. Families flourish when they help each generation—parents, children, and grandchildren—live their lives, on their own and together, as flourishing individuals. Giving is at the core of flourishing. As the researchers at the University of California–Berkeley's Greater Good Project have found, people are generally happiest when they have the choice to spend quality time with loved ones, feel gratitude for gifts received, and do something good for others.[1] The goal is simple. The difficulties come in reaching it.

Anything so important to family flourishing is also central to parenting. Many parents recognize that gifts of money or property can affect their children's growth and development. But family giving extends well beyond money or stocks or bonds or other material things. It involves giving time, care, advice, and love as well as freedom and room to grow. Parenting itself can be understood as a many-faceted form of giving—one that, due to its complexity, requires the capacity for humility and self-forgiveness.

Understood this way, parenting and family giving go hand in hand. Giving can support a family's core work—preparing each generation to be free and flourishing individuals—by helping children feel loved, cared for, and ultimately secure in their own lives and livelihood. It can also complicate that work, because gifts may make recipients feel obliged to or dependent on the giver.

As a result, we will continually ask in this book, *how can we give and receive in ways to enhance growth and freedom rather than subsidize dependency and entitlement?*

Adele and Albert's situation shows that silence, as tempting as it is, will not guarantee success in family giving any more than in the rest of parenting. Actions may speak louder than words, but they cannot speak without words. If you do not explain your deeds, others will do so—and perhaps ascribe motivations you never intended. Giving will not be all that it can be or that we want it to be without thoughtful communication.

Parents and grandparents want to help their children and grandchildren become free and flourishing individuals. They want them to be happy rather than to suffer. Likewise, children and grandchildren want to be happy and to grow, remaining connected to their parents but also becoming independent and free. Family giving—understood in the broadest sense and prepared by reflection and communication—can play an integral role in achieving these goals.

That is why we wrote this book.

Question:
What has complicated your own discussions with your children or grandchildren about gifts you have made or plan to make to them?

Note

1. For more on the Greater Good Project's research, visit their website at http://greatergood.berkeley.edu.

Chapter 2

The Spirit of the Gift

While many people think of giving as having to do with birthdays, holidays, and perhaps end-of-the-year tax planning, we think it is much bigger than that: Family giving is integral to flourishing. What makes us think that family giving can have such power and impact? The key is what we call the *spirit of the gift*.

The spirit of a gift reveals itself first in the intention of the giver. The intention first launches the meteor-gift. It is the answer to the question, why are you giving this to me?

But intention is just the beginning of the story. People like to say, "It's the thought that counts." It certainly does, but it is not the only thing that counts. Many gifts also carry qualities that transcend the thoughts (or thoughtlessness) of the giver. That is one of the wonderful things about gifts: They are not limited to their givers' plans. Instead, gifts often take on lives of their own.

Consider a few examples. A Christmas gift of a toy truck to an eager child carries with it the spirit of playfulness. The gift of a grandfather's Marine Corp ring to a grandson embodies courage and honor in the face of danger. The present of a fine pen to a college graduate carries with it the spirit of encouragement and seriousness about work and career. The gift of an engagement ring to a fiancée expresses the hope for an unbroken union. And the gift of a stuffed animal to an elderly patient helps people hold onto softness and gentleness even in the face of death. In each of these cases, the spirit of the gift includes the feelings, thoughts, and actions that the gift itself excites, whether or not the giver intended them.

Because of the life that gifts possess, their spirit has an additional, social element, which ties together givers and recipients in a profound way. Anthropology teaches that in many societies— whether among the Native Americans of the Northwest or the tribes of Polynesia—gifts were understood, quite literally, to bear a spirit or soul that both givers and recipients must acknowledge and respect.[1] To keep that spirit alive, recipients had to become givers themselves and return the gift or give it forward. If they did not, the spirit of the unreciprocated gift would turn against its possessor. This understanding of the spirit of the gift survives in non-Western societies that have a strong connection to traditional views. For example, in China and many other Eastern nations, an inheritance is not just property. Instead, it embodies the spirit of the ancestors who accumulated the fortune as well as the spirit of those who preserved and passed it on. With each giving and receiving, the gift accumulates greater spirit.

One does not need to be traditional Chinese, Kwakiutl, or Trobriand to understand the spirit of the gift. Nor do you have to be "spiritual" or "new age." If you have ever made a particularly good gift, you know how alive you felt in doing so. If you have seen your gift ignored or misused, you know the feeling of loss, not just to the recipient or to yourself but also to the very spirit of the gift. (In Chapter 3, we will see how that sense of loss often plays itself out in something we call grantor's remorse.) If you have ever made a gift out of guilt, you know that, in some way, the spirit feels tainted. Conversely, if you have received a meaningful gift, you know that you have received something not just material but spiritual. With this spirit comes the desire to receive the gift respectfully and, most likely, to use it for the benefit of others.

The spirit of the gift, we believe, arises from the natural struggle between entropy—the force of decline, diminishment, and destruction—and growth or generativity.[2] So often in our lives stale forms of thought and behavior contribute to entropy. Gifts offered as mere subsidies, to maintain the existing state of things, actually foster decline. How many times have these subsidies undermined the well-being they were meant to maintain! In contrast, gifts that seek to transform and enhance often generate new life.

What happens when a gift lacks spirit? In such cases, the gift becomes not a gift but a transfer. A transfer is the movement of a lifeless object from one person to another, a figure from my accounting column to yours. That's what happens in most business exchanges. That's also what Adele and Albert found was happening in their family: The annual exclusion gifts had ceased to bear any spirit and had become mere transfers. That's what happens when family members find themselves unable to speak about or realize the fullness of their gifts to one another.

For example, we know a woman who decided to send her 20-something son a $13,000 annual exclusion check. She did not know what to say to him about it, so she just told him that he must deposit it right away before year-end. The next year she decided to talk with him more fully about the annual gift. She mentioned that she had sent such a check last year. He replied, "You did?" She reminded him and he recalled, "Oh, yes, the check I had to get to the bank right away." In the absence of communication, all that had stuck out to him was the need to deposit it quickly. He remembered only the transaction. There was no spirit.

But what happened next is just as important. Because the mother had opened up the lines of communication, the son had a

chance to think for a moment and respond to her offer. He gratefully but firmly said, "You don't need to give me this. You have
given me enough already." He wanted to move ahead with his
life independently. They had a great discussion and, in the end,
decided that the mother would deposit her annual gift in a fund
for her son's possible graduate education. In this way, what started
as a transfer ended up becoming a true gift. Similarly, we hope
this book helps ensure that your giving and receiving fosters spirit
and does not result merely in transfers.

Entropy, generativity, subsidy, and *enhancement* may sound like
abstract terms, but they become concrete realities in family giving.
Another brief story may make this point clearer. A number of years
ago, one of us (Jay Hughes) was sitting in his law office in New
York when he received a call from a dear friend and client whom
we will call Leo. Leo was trustee of a family trust that benefited a
number of his family members. Leo and Jay had long agreed that
the trust should make only distributions that were enhancing. They
had also agreed that any distribution that was a subsidy (i.e., a mere
transfer) was likely to be harmful to the recipient. Leo sincerely
wanted to do well by anyone he touched; he was also parsimonious
by nature. He enjoyed tweaking Jay on this issue because Jay is by
nature expansive in his view of what is enhancing.

So, on the phone that day Leo said, "This time I have you!
I know you will agree that this request by a beneficiary for a distribution, if fulfilled, would be a subsidy, so I shouldn't agree to
make it."

Jay replied, "Well, okay, but who is asking for what?"

"My niece is making the request, and she wants a cleaning
lady once a week! Clearly, no one needs such a person, so this
must be a subsidy, and I certainly should say no."

"Really?" Jay replied. "Am I correct that your niece has a
husband who works very hard and long hours? Am I also correct
that she has two sons who are teenagers and have very busy lives
but don't drive yet? And doesn't she teach school full time?"

"Well, yes," said Leo. "That is all true."

"And isn't she very frugal and has almost never requested anything of the trust?"

"Well, yes," Leo agreed again.

"Do you believe that your niece has any time for herself—any time to savor sitting down with a cup of tea without someone else's agenda taking over, any time just to chat with her husband or her sons? Might a cleaning lady give her a few hours each week to be with herself or her loved ones without distraction?"

"Oh, dear," Leo responded. "I hadn't considered all that. I'll approve the request." He then went on to say, "I've learned that what counts as enhancing depends on the unique circumstances in which each beneficiary finds herself and the entire system in which she exists. I've also learned that being an enhancing trustee requires true wisdom!"

The spirit of the gift encompasses the intention of the giver, the life of the gift itself, and the generative flow from givers to recipients by which recipients become new givers in turn. This flow is what we call, in the language of anthropology, the cycle of the gift. All these things follow from understanding gifts not just as embodying financial value but also as carrying spirit. The spirit distinguishes between transfers that subsidize and gifts that enhance, between entropy and growth.

Where the Spirit Leads

The power of spirit in family giving is palpable. It teaches us that giving is about much more than the objects given. Often people focus on the object—whether money, a piece of jewelry, a toy, or a new car. Spirit moves our attention away from the things and to the people involved in the giving. More precisely, it draws our attention to the activities those people engage in and the connections they have with each other.

Such distinctions have important practical results. For example, when we first met Adele and Albert, they had begun to wonder if there was something wrong not just with their descendants but also with their gifts. Was the amount of each check too small? Too big? Should they include a personalized note with each one? They thought that something was missing in the gifts themselves.

Focusing on the spirit of the gift gave Adele and Albert the permission to experience the joy of giving, and it helped them see the situation in a deeper way. They turned from these doubts or questions about their gifts to reflection on their family. In particular, they found themselves thinking seriously about (and eventually talking seriously with) their children and grandchildren, their recipients. Who were they, and what did each one need? These questions led to conversations, which gave Adele and Albert an opportunity to share their core values with their children and grandchildren: the values of hard work, giving, and education. They truly were able to give more than money. And their children and grandchildren were more open to receive. Adele and Albert taught us a valuable lesson: As important as giving wisely is, it is all the more important to reflect on recipients and to prepare them to receive wisely. Many times the power of the spirit of the gift reveals itself—or is quashed—depending on the state of soul of the recipient.

More broadly, we believe that giving with spirit can help families address some of the core concerns of contemporary society. As people spread out geographically and take up many different occupations and lifestyles, they interact less as members of a family and more as individuals. Personal freedom may increase, but the feeling of connection often weakens. Many family members also worry that consumerism makes their families more physically comfortable but spiritually poorer and may even undermine the very meaning of family. We see the spirit of the gift as a crucial response to these real concerns.

Finally, the spirit and the cycle of the gift can also help us understand our own individual development. As we will discuss in Chapter 4, each of us goes through a life cycle of receiving, giving, or giving back, and ultimately receiving once more. Recognizing where your children or grandchildren and you yourself are in this cycle is crucial to giving well. The connection between the social cycle of the gift (the cycle from giver to recipient to future recipient) and the cycle embodied in individual development is rooted, again, in the nature of things. As a society and as individuals—in our families and in our bodies—we constantly flow between entropy and growth.

We give you this understanding of the spirit of the gift as something to reflect on. We hope that in reading further you find that spirit in your life and family. That way you may truly take it to heart and make it something you can give to yourself and others in turn.

Question:
What are two examples of gifts you made that left you feeling joy?

Notes

1. The classic evidence appears in Marcel Mauss, *The Gift: The Form and Reason for Exchange in Archaic Societies*, trans. W. D. Halls (New York: W.W. Norton and Co., 1990). See also Lewis Hyde, *The Gift: Imagination and the Erotic Life of Property* (New York: Vintage Books, 1983), particularly Part 1.

2. For more on these terms, see Jay Hughes's *Family: The Compact among Generations* (New York: Bloomberg Press, 2007), 31–46.

THE WHO OF GIVING

Chapter 3

Becoming
a Wise Giver

In practice, givers and their advisors often give much of their attention to the mechanics of giving: the strategies, plans, and nuts and bolts of various transactions. All of these mechanics belong to the question of "how," as in How can I minimize taxes? or How can I protect my assets? Such questions are usually in the service of quantity: getting the most bang for the buck.

But before the *how* questions come the *who* questions, which focus on quality. And the most important who is the recipient. If you are a parent or grandparent, you probably already have a pretty good idea of those people to whom you wish to give. But who are these people *really*? Who are they as individuals? What are their individual strengths and weaknesses? What are their individual dreams?

Giving well thus requires understanding your recipients. But understanding your recipients requires understanding yourself, as a giver and as a human being. Therefore, we will turn first, in this chapter, to understanding yourself as a giver. In Chapter 4 we will return to the question of understanding recipients.

To begin the task of understanding yourself, we encourage you to consider what your wealth truly is. To do that, we suggest you spend a moment reflecting. Make some space in your head and heart to read the following paragraphs and reflect on the thoughts and feelings they provoke. The primary question to consider in this exercise is, What is your wealth *really*?

Close your eyes and think about your most joyful moments, past or present. Visualize those moments as fully as you can, feeling what it is like just to be there, in those moments. Reflect on what you are doing, how you are feeling, who you are with, and what you are saying. Now, ask yourself, What is my true wealth?

This simple exercise can have profound consequences. It has the potential to make clear, in a visual way, what you consider your true wealth. Keep the results of this exercise in mind as you read and reflect on the ideas that follow.

Know Thyself

How can we prepare ourselves to give wisely to our family members, that is, in such a way as to encourage their growth, freedom, and flourishing? In the ancient world, when people felt unsure what to do about a serious matter, they did not seek out consultants or therapists or self-help books. Instead, they traveled to the Oracle of Delphi. As a result, a lot of people ended up standing around the temple door. To inspire those who were waiting, some philanthropists had two inscriptions carved over the doorway. We will focus first on the more famous of the two, which reads, in Greek, *Gnothi Sauton*, which means, "Know thyself."

It is an odd saying. After all, some seekers had traveled hundreds of miles to get an answer, and they were being told that they had

had their answers, all this time, inside themselves. But this simple inscription has had perhaps more impact than any other philanthropic act since. Socrates based the enterprise of Western philosophy on it. And Sigmund Freud returned to it in the late nineteenth century as the foundation for modern psychology.

"Know thyself" is the true starting point for discernment. Everything you think, plan, and do is shaped by your experiences and beliefs. To clarify your thoughts, plans, and actions you must first know yourself. We refer to this process as "clearing your lenses." It is impossible to see anything—including what is best for your recipients—without clear lenses.

This process differs for each of us, but questions are often critical sources for guidance for our individual journeys. We have offered one already: What is my true wealth? Another question to ask is, what really matters to me—and why? It is an extremely powerful question—and not an easy one to answer. Every year a friend of ours who serves as dean of religious studies for a leading university invites a distinguished guest to lecture to all the undergraduates and share his or her answer to this one question. Year after year, the lecturers report that it was the most difficult lecture they ever gave. And year after year, students respond that it was one of the most important lectures they ever heard. If you were asked to give this lecture, what would you say?

Here are a couple other related questions to consider: What are your dreams? What are your ultimate aspirations? In a recent study of family leaders with at least $25 million in net worth, researchers asked, "What is your ultimate goal or deepest aspiration?" The most prevalent answer did not involve professional or financial success; rather, it was, "To be a good parent."[1]

Once you have clarified what your dreams are, ask yourself, have I shared those dreams with the intended recipients of my gifts? To be successful at family giving, givers need to be honest with recipients—and themselves—about the expectations they attach to their gifts. Careful gifts may *promote* freedom, but the spirit of the gift teaches us that no gift by itself is ever completely free. It is the nature of that spirit to bring with it a sense of expectation. What expectations are built into your gifts? That the recipients will thank you? Join the business? Succeed on their own? Keep up your estate? Spend weekends and vacations with you? A wise advisor we know asked a client who was itching to make a gift to take advantage of a changing tax law, "What effect do you want this gift to *really* have?" That question moved the conversation away from quantities and toward quality, from form toward function. It led ultimately to more mindful planning.

To recap, the Delphic Oracle teaches that the first step in giving well is self-knowledge. That knowledge can be gained through reflecting on questions such as, What is my wealth? What really matters to me—and why? and What are my dreams? In the context of family wealth and family giving, additional important questions are, To what degree have I shared my dreams with my children or grandchildren? What do I expect in return for my gifts? and What effect do I really want my wealth to have, now and in the future?

Questions to Consider:
What is my true wealth?
What really matters to me and why?
What are my dreams?
What are my ultimate aspirations?
Have I shared my dreams with the intended recipients of my gifts?
What do I expect to come from my gifts?
What effects do I truly want them to have?

How Much?

When it comes to questions about giving, perhaps the most common one we hear from parents with wealth is, "How much is enough for me to give or to leave to my children and grandchildren?" which people usually shorten to "How much is enough?"

We have worked with families in which enough was $10 million per child. Others with whom we have worked have pegged the number at over $25 million. Still others, despite their great wealth, have limited enough to a million dollars or less. But the question of how much is enough never admits of an easy, numerical answer. Once we were talking to a gathering of CEOs when one of them interrupted us. "Fine," he grumbled, "I get the point. Money complicates family life. But how about you just answer the darn question we're all wondering about: How much is enough?"

One of us turned to him and said, "Seven million dollars."

He looked a bit taken aback. "Why seven million?" he asked.

"Well, why not?" was the answer. "If you need to have a number, seven million seems as good as any other."

At this response, his frown vanished and he gave a hearty laugh. He recognized that no number alone would be the right answer for his family. He moved from an unreflective focus on quantity to a mindful awareness of the importance of quality.

Even though it's a quantitative question, thinking through How much is enough? can help you clear your lenses. To help sort out this question, we find it helpful to distinguish three things: How much money do you want in order to *live*? How much to *give*? and How much to *leave*? The first question is not, how much is enough for my children? Rather, it is, How much is enough *for me*?

Answering the question, How much do I require to live? means thinking about your own needs and your own dreams— qualitative matters. If they include maintaining multiple residences and vehicles and supporting a lavish lifestyle, then your number will be large. Such needs and dreams may mean you will have less to give or leave. Or, conversely, your tastes may mean that you will seek all the more to give to your children, to help subsidize the lifestyle to which you have accustomed them and believe they should have.

The question of how much money you want to live on leads quickly to the question of how much you want to give. When it comes to giving during your lifetime, the basic gift many parents offer to their children is education. Since the beginning of the twentieth century, millions of parents have saved or gone into debt to pay for college. This is the most common form of lifetime wealth transfer, and parents do it because they believe a quality education will help their children lead a better life than they had. In contrast, before the Industrial Revolution, parents would commonly transfer their trade to their children and leave them their tools or their shop when they died.[2] Giving a child a trade or an education is a qualitative rather than quantitative gift, which explains why many parents are willing to pay almost anything for tuition.

The old form of wealth transfer promoted social stability: families would follow the same trade generation after generation. The new form promotes social progress: each generation seeks to do materially better than the one before. That is a clear challenge for children of parents who have created significant wealth. For such a system also encourages social fluidity. A minority of people in the top 20 percent or bottom 20 percent of wealth remain there from one generation to the next.[3] A glance at the famous Forbes 400 list reveals that only 24 members of the original list (published in 1982) still hold a place in it in 2012—and only three of those (Warren Buffett and Charles and David Koch) remain in the top 20.[4] Nor is the fluidity of wealth a new phenomenon. As the American novelist Herman Melville put it in the 1852, "In our cities families rise and burst like bubbles in a vat."[5]

If you are a parent with wealth, you try—as do all parents—to give your children the best education you can. Beyond that, you face a choice. Do you give your children more during their lives, in order to help them try to hold on to your standard of living? Or do you consciously give your children less, so as not to inadvertently subsidize an unsustainable standard of living? These questions point to an even more fundamental qualitative choice: Do you want your children to take your standard of living as their own?

These questions connect closely with the third consideration: How much is enough for me to *leave* my children or grandchildren? Many parents like the idea of giving everything they can during their lifetimes so that they can see their descendants enjoy their gifts. Of course, doing so may leave you dependent on your children. Shakespeare's *King Lear* and Balzac's *Father Goriot* suggest that such a plan requires careful consideration of your needs and the character of your children.

As attractive as giving it all away during your lifetime may seem, many parents still feel drawn to leaving their children bequests. In literature and in life, many parents say, "I just want to leave my children something—perhaps more than I got from my parents." This desire is a powerful one. It may look purely quantitative: I want to give them more. But in its way, it is a perfect expression of the social cycle of the gift: just as I received from my parents, so I want to give to my children, and I want the gift to have grown in my hands, rather than to have diminished. The moment of passing also seems important: it is precisely in the face of death that we want to see gifts grow.[6] Not the quantities involved but the presence of the spirit of the gift in the face of mortality gives this impulse its power.

This brief consideration of these three questions—How much is enough for me to live? To give? To leave?—shows how wise givers can break the puzzling quantitative question, How much is enough for my kids? into more manageable qualitative queries. It also shows how important it is to recognize that the first questions to address focus not on others but on *you*. It is crucial to separate out what you think is best for your children and grandchildren from what you think is right for you. How much do you want to live on?

Do you want your standard of living to be their standard of living? Do you want what you received from your parents to be the measure of what your children receive from you? These questions can be tough but also freeing. They may release you from weighty expectations that you have imposed on yourself. That is why mindful givers will not just jump to focusing on others. They will take the time first to clear their own lenses.

Guilt and Remorse

In the interest of such lens clearing, we want to touch on two other related topics: guilt giving and grantor's remorse.

Guilt is a powerful motivation in many people's giving. Sometimes parents make such gifts because they feel that they have not given their children other, more important things (such as love, affection, or time). They seek to make up for that loss with material things. Guilt about a divorce may have similar effects. Something similar happens in the philanthropic world when donors feel guilty about the source of their funds and hope to expunge that guilt through their charity. At times, charitable recipients (and children) may even play upon the giver's guilt to exact bigger gifts. Another form of guilt arises when professionals tell clients, "You would be crazy not to take full advantage of these loopholes in the tax code!" Who wants to be seen as crazy or to miss out on profitable advice? Nonetheless, guilt motivates the lowest sort of giving on Maimonides's ladder, the grudging sort.

Guilt is powerful, and it is ultimately destructive. Guilt is not a pure emotion like anger, sadness, fear, or joy. Guilt is a hybrid built from a mix of the others. No one takes joy in a gift triggered by guilt. The gift only reminds the giver of the perceived fault or failing. And the recipient knows, at least intuitively, that the gift was not for him or her but for the giver's wounded ego. Because they are ultimately self-directed, gifts made from guilt sap spirit rather than enhance life. Because it hurts to think closely about such gifts, guilt usually leads to unreflective giving. And gifts prompted by guilt easily become mere transfers.

As a result, such gifts are often connected to the phenomenon of grantor's remorse. Grantor's remorse can also arise in situations unrelated to guilt. It is the giver's version of buyer's remorse. For example, we met a couple who had successfully transferred most of their business interests, at very low tax costs, to trusts for their young children. They were not feeling guilty. They were quite pleased with this move, because when the business soon popped in value, tens of millions of dollars went to these trusts tax free. We congratulated them on this tactic but then began a conversation with them focused on the question, how do you feel about your children each having eight-figure wealth in 10 years? At that point their faces fell. They realized their gift was irrevocable. To use an image we shared earlier, they felt terrible about the enormous *meteor* they had sent sailing toward their young children and the effects its impact might have.

Grantor's remorse is often a consequence of making unreflective gifts. This couple was focused on beating the taxman, and they did so very effectively. Grantor's remorse can also flow even from thoughtful gifts. This couple, after all, believed they should benefit their children, as any parent does. But they had not truly asked themselves what that benefit would look like or how to bring it about. Their children were very young. No one knew the kind of individuals they would someday become. Less focus on tax strategies and more mindfulness about themselves and others would have saved them this remorse. As it turned out, we worked with them over several years to prepare themselves and their children for their gift. The preparation helped them turn their remorse into a responsible plan of preparation with very positive results.

Clearing your lenses means acknowledging when guilt may be in the driver's seat. It also anticipates what actions may cause remorse. In these ways, we can see that self-knowledge ultimately prepares you to more effectively consider the welfare of others, which is hard to do when your own emotions get in the way. Knowing thyself is a key step in discerning how to benefit others.

Nothing Too Much

As we mentioned at the beginning of this chapter, above the door to the Delphic Oracle were two inscriptions. One was "Know thyself," which we offered as the first step in giving wisely. The other was, in Greek, *Meden Agan*, which means "Nothing too much." This is, for us, a practical rule of thumb for giving well.

At the most basic level, "Nothing too much" means not giving when you do not have enough information. In much of this chapter, we have encouraged understanding yourself, your dreams, and your expectations. In the chapters that follow, we discuss the importance not only of understanding your recipients but also of communicating with your spouse, children, and grandchildren to build that understanding. Understanding takes time. Before you have it, you may want to refrain from making major gifts, for the simple reason that you do not have the data you need on the people who will be affected. The saying "Nothing too much" goes hand in hand with the old medical injunction "First, do no harm."

"Nothing too much" also reminds us of spirit. A gift without spirit constitutes "too much." The absence of quality undermines even the greatest quantity. Recall Adele and Albert's checks, from Chapter 1, or the young man who thought the $13,000 was something he just had to deposit in the bank, from Chapter 2. If you cannot articulate the purpose or meaning of a gift given to a specific recipient, you are likely giving too much. Ask yourself, when do I feel most alive when giving? If you do not feel alive in making a gift, it probably contains too much money and not enough spirit. If guilt is your motivator, then spirit will soon disappear. You can also ask yourself, how anxious am I feeling about this gift? If you feel significant anxiety, then you may be right to hesitate.

Many donors readily apply these practical guidelines in their philanthropic giving. They would not dream of giving to a charitable institution without clarifying the purpose and uses of the gift. They would want to articulate, as clearly as possible, the spirit that motivates the gift. They would certainly not want to make a gift that harms the charitable institution. The same attitude can prove a helpful guide in giving to family.

Factors that contribute to giving wisely include coming to know yourself—asking what your true wealth is and what really matters to you and why. It also involves separating your understanding of your recipients' needs from your sense of your own needs, including what you would like to see happen or how guilty you may feel. Finally, discerned giving involves using the precept of "Nothing too much" to help move attention from the quantity or timing of the gift to its spirit—the sense of activity or flourishing that frees givers and makes them feel truly alive. It helps us remember that such gifts are much more than money.

Question:
Earlier we shared the image of the gift as a "meteor," flying from giver to recipient. What is in your meteor?

Notes

1. The study is entitled "The Joys and Dilemmas of Wealth," undertaken by the Boston College Center on Wealth and Philanthropy and funded by the Bill and Melinda Gates Foundation and Abbot Downing, a Wells Fargo business. For a discussion of initial results, see Graeme Wood, "The Secret Fears of the Super Rich," *Atlantic Monthly*, April 2011.

2. See Peter Dobkin Hall and George E. Marcus, "Why Should Men Leave Great Fortunes to Their Children? Dynasty and Inheritance in America," in *Inheritance and Wealth in America*, ed. Robert K. Miller Jr. and Stephen J. McNamee (New York: Plenum Press, 1998), 139-172.

3. See Bruce Bartlett, "Wealth, Mobility, Inheritance, and the Estate Tax," National Center for Policy Analysis Policy Report No. 235, July 2000.

4. The 24 are Herbert Allen (investment banking), Phil Anschutz (invest-
   ments), Sid Bass (oil), Stephen Bechtel (construction), Donald Bren
   (real estate), Warren Buffett (investments), Anne Chambers (media),
   Gordon Getty (oil), Henry Hillman (investments), Ray Hunt (oil),
   Kirk Kerkorian (investments), Phil Knight (retail), Charles and David
   Koch (diversified products), Leonard and Ronald Lauder (cosmetics),
   Patrick McGovern (media), David Murdock (real estate), Donald and
   Samuel Newhouse (publishing), Ross Perot (computer services), David
   Rockefeller (banking), Ted Turner (cable television), and Leslie Wexner
   (retail). While some of these individuals inherited wealth, none of them
   attained their current level of wealth without considerable effort and
   acumen.

5. Herman Melville, *Pierre: Or the Ambiguities* (New York: Harper Collins,
   1995 [1852]), 13.

6. See Lewis Hyde, *The Gift: Imagination and the Erotic Life of Property*
   (New York: Vintage, 1983), particularly Chapter 3.

Chapter 4

Receiving Wisely

One of the most important parts of giving well is to understand who your recipients are. As discussed in Chapter 3, to do so requires first clearing your lenses. As we will see in this chapter, it also requires empathy, on the part of both the giver and the recipient. Understanding comes more easily for some than for others. The giver and the recipient may spend plenty of time together and enjoy a close relationship. Or age, geography, family commitments, business, or old baggage may all get in the way.

But understanding and empathy alone do not make a gift successful. Giving well involves receiving well, which depends on the recipient's ability to integrate the gift into her life. As one of Adele and Albert's daughters-in-law said, their gifts felt to her like a meteor that rocked her world. Her words reflect the reality that many families intuitively know: Even the best-intentioned gifts can cause discomfort and pain rather than joy and growth. Receiving wisely demands not only understanding but also integrating the gift into one's life. Both givers and recipients have important roles to play in preparing for that integration.

A Bad Investment?

What makes it hard for givers to understand and empathize with recipients? There are obstacles that go deeper than geography or busyness. A short story may help make the point.

We met once with a successful entrepreneur in his 70s, whom we will call Mike. Mike had just finished signing his estate plan, which would transfer much of his fortune to his children and grandchildren. He seemed a bit down, so we asked him how he was doing. Mike shook his head and said, "I'm glad I can give my children and grandchildren so much. But I can't give them the one thing I valued most in my life: the chance to make it on their own." Rather than feeling generous, he felt that he was depriving them.

In the developed world, particularly in the United States, nearly 80 percent of all wealth has been created within the lifetime of the present wealth holders, usually through success in business. When wealth creators meet with us to discuss estate plans or gifts, they bring the experience of struggle and striving. They know how painful such struggles often are. But they also know the rewards, emotional and financial. They worry that their gifts to their children or grandchildren will keep their descendants from experiencing the satisfaction of making it on their own. They worry, as Mike put it, that they are making a bad investment.

The Land of Wealth

Besides *self-made* versus *heir*, a distinction that we find helpful is that of *immigrants to* and *natives in* the land of wealth. Immigrants do not grow up with wealth, so it feels to them like another world, with its own customs, rules, and language. Immigrants to wealth often either try to assimilate and outdo the natives or maintain a version of the old country by driving old cars or living in modest homes. (Compare a McMansion with Warren Buffett's Omaha house.) Natives, in contrast, grew up in the atmosphere of wealth and likely know nothing else. While immigrants often feel confident in their abilities but uncomfortable in their new suits, natives often feel comfortable amid wealth but unsure of their own abilities to make their way in the world themselves.*

*For more on this distinction, see Grubman, Jaffe, and Whitaker, "Immigration to the Land of Wealth," *Private Wealth Magazine* (March–April, 2009).

No doubt gifts may have negative consequences for recipients. Recipients may be left feeling confused, guilty, angry, and afraid. As a result, some of them deny, hoard, or consume their gifts. A gift may upset one's identity. As one young man said to us, "I sometimes wonder am I me or am I this trust? Who would I be without it?" It is no surprise that *heir* is not a positive word in the modern world. From Benjamin Franklin's *Poor Richard* in the eighteenth century to entrepreneurs such as Steve Jobs, our society celebrates the self-made man or woman.

Mike prided himself in being self-made. Still, as we talked with Mike, he gladly acknowledged the great debt that he owed to his own parents in helping him make a good start in life and business. He also acknowledged that many friends promoted him and his work.

In fact, Mike and the rest of us all receive untold numbers of goods from others. We may refine our smarts, our drive, and our endurance, for example, but we do not invent them. The same goes for the learning we get from teachers or the connections we receive from family and friends or the inspiration we receive from who knows where. In truth, we are all heirs.

As Mike reflected on how much he had received, he began to feel differently about his children and grandchildren and about his gifts. He let go of the gloomy view that giving is a bad investment. Instead, mindful of how much others had invested in him, he began to wonder how he could best *invest* in his family members. His estate plan was done, but his work as a giver had just begun. Mike accepted the awareness that he, too, was a recipient. As a result, he could better see the world through his own recipients' eyes and begin the journey to add spirit to his giving.

The Psychological Stages of Giving

The work of discernment, which is at the core of mindful giving, begins with the search for understanding. What does understanding recipients involve? How do you answer the questions, Who *really* are the prospective recipients of my gifts? What are their true needs? and What are their fears and dreams?

The first thing to reflect on is temperament. Temperament goes deeper than values. It appears early in a child's life, even before the teenage years. Children in the same family may have widely different temperaments. One child may be cautious and shy, another confident. One may be a spender, another a hoarder. One may be critical of herself, another judgmental of others. One may be open to the world and another defensive and protective. Temperament is mysterious but powerful.

Age is another crucial consideration. In the past few decades, psychology has revealed how children of different ages possess different cognitive and emotional skills and face different developmental challenges. When we talk about giving with families, we often find it helpful to ground the discussion in the thought of Erik Erikson.

Erikson was a psychoanalyst and a student of Sigmund Freud's daughter Anna. He took traditional Freudian thought on childhood development and expanded it to include eight stages, encompassing the whole of human life. He believed that to progress from one stage to the next each of us must face and resolve a conflict characteristic to that stage. Parents often find an awareness of Erickson's stages to be a helpful guide in their parenting journey. Erikson's stages are noted below, each with a brief description. As you read them, reflect on yourself, your children, and your grandchildren, recognizing that the stages are not simply linear. Sometimes people go back and reexperience an earlier stage and then move forward to embrace the next.

Developmental Stages

Trust versus mistrust. Birth to one year: The goal of this stage is for the infant to gain a sense of trust in his environment. The infant needs maximum comfort with minimal uncertainty to trust himself, others, and the environment. Clearly, desperate economic circumstances can impact children negatively at this stage. So, too, can great wealth, if it means that infants and young children experience care from a revolving door of nannies or other caregivers.

Autonomy versus shame and doubt. Ages two to three: The goal of this stage is for the toddler to feel a sense of separateness from his parents and to start to become an autonomous individual with a sense of self. The toddler's work is to master the physical environment while maintaining self-esteem.

Initiative versus guilt. Ages four to five: The goal of this stage is for the preschooler to begin to initiate, not just imitate, activities. Learning to persevere and experience a sense of accomplishment is the core challenge of this stage. This is the time when children often begin to make comparisons with each other's family houses, cars, and so on.

Industry versus inferiority. Age six to puberty: The goal of this stage is for the school-age child to develop a sense of self-worth by refining skills and interests. The core challenge is to develop the desire to feel useful, to be motivated to accomplish through diligence and focus. Children at this stage are ready (and often eager) to start learning about allowances or earning money through helpful activities.

Identity versus role confusion. Adolescence: The goal of this stage is for the adolescent to begin to integrate many roles (child, sibling, student, athlete, and worker) into a self-image. The challenge for the adolescent is to develop his own identity amid peer pressure and to feel capable of learning to master life successfully as an individual. Traditional estate planning, with payouts from trusts at age 21, often raise parents' (and children's) anxieties, because the money often starts flowing just as the recipients are most confused about their lives.

Intimacy versus isolation. Young adulthood: The goal of this stage is for the young adult to learn to establish meaningful connections with others and make personal commitments to another as a spouse, parent, or partner. Again, traditional estate planning can intensify this conflict by demanding that young adults focus on their family of origin (its wealth or its business) just as they are naturally trying to make their own way in the world.

Generativity versus stagnation. Middle adulthood: The goal for this stage is for the adult to find satisfaction by giving back through productivity in career, family, and civic interests. Growing a business or one's own career is often a key endeavor at this stage.

Integrity versus despair. Later adulthood: The goal for this stage is for the older adult to review life accomplishments, deal with loss, and find purpose and peace. Family giving may give parents or grandparents an occasion to work towards these goals.

Erikson's thought allows discerning givers to better understand recipients and themselves. As we mentioned in Chapter 2, we believe it is also possible to understand givers' and recipients' development in terms of giving and receiving—an individual cycle of the gift. To be specific, in addition to Erikson's stages of development, we have found that healthy people usually go through at least three (sometimes four) stages of life with regard to giving. If discerning givers and recipients are to understand themselves, it is important also to keep these stages in mind.

In the first stage of the life of giving and receiving, from our childhood through our late 20s or early 30s, most people are fundamentally receivers. The focus is on ourselves: our physical and emotional growth, our education and learning, the beginnings of our romantic attachments, the start of our careers, and perhaps even the beginning of our family lives. People in this first stage are sometimes eager to learn about giving, say, through charitable activities at school or at home. It is important to expose children and young adults to the value of giving and particularly to the value of giving thanks. Doing so helps children acknowledge the power of the spirit of the gift in their lives. However, at this stage their true work is to receive well: to learn from teachers, parents, and mentors; to form their own values; and to develop their talents.

In the middle stage of life, from our early 30s to our early 60s, most people are focused on integrating and building on what they have received. We build (and sometimes rebuild) our families and our careers. We build a connection to a larger community. People in this stage may naturally begin to give, for they have started to create something of their own (wealth, skills, knowledge, connections, etc.) from which to give.

In the third stage of life, from our 60s into old age, most people move from building and producing toward what has come to be called, following Erikson, generativity. We look for ways to reconnect with our children and to come to know our grandchildren. We transition from doing our own work toward mentoring others. The main desire is to give back.

In the very last stage of life, in old age, people return once more to receiving. Often that means receiving physical care as well as emotional support and connection. In this way, just as gifts inspire a circular movement in society (of giving, receiving, and giving back), so, too, there is a cycle of the gift in individual life itself.

Keeping this cycle in mind is especially important for parents or grandparents of children in the first stage. It helps to remember that they are at a very different point in life than you are. *While your focus may be on giving or giving back, theirs is likely on themselves. This does not make them selfish. It makes them human.*

For example, we have met many philanthropists who have worried aloud about the next generation and its willingness to give. One woman in her 50s who spoke this way to us complained in particular about her 23-year-old daughter, who was just starting her career: the mother felt the daughter was not sufficiently committed to the family's philanthropy. We helped her see that her daughter was doing the work that was developmentally appropriate for her at that point in her life—just as she, her mother, was for her own stage.

Giving and the Work Ethic

Our overall goal is to enhance life by giving and receiving with spirit. We have seen how important it is to remember that we are all heirs of one sort or another. We have also seen the importance of taking into account our recipients' (and our own) temperament, age, and stage of development in the individual cycle of the gift.

A key concern that many would-be givers voice about recipients is, How can I give without undermining my children's or grandchildren's work ethic, sense of autonomy, and pride in their own accomplishments? (This was the question lurking behind Mike's worries about his gifts.) This question has its twin in a concern that many recipients express: How can I receive from my parents or grandparents without the money taking over my sense of purpose in life and making me feel guilty or dependent?

These questions are not just about work but rather about the relationship between work, life, and money. After all, most parents do not want their children to work at jobs they hate just to earn a large salary. Likewise, most parents do not want to subsidize idleness. What matters are the work and the life, not the money—the activity, not the resource. As Sigmund Freud taught, to live well, the two main tasks for any individual are to learn to love and to labor. He also said that our greatest struggles are around love, work, and money.

Children in wealthy families face some additional complexities in these struggles. Practically, they may not need to work to earn their bread—and as a result they may miss out in learning what work is. In contrast, as the philosopher Rousseau put it, "The poor man does not need to be educated. His station gives him a compulsory education."[1] In addition, because they have the means to do so, many affluent parents encourage their children to hold out for meaningful rather than menial work. On one level, this advice makes sense: Why spend the summer cleaning the locker room at the club when you could be improving your game with the tennis pro? But by setting their children's eyes on such a lofty goal, parents may make it all the more difficult for their children to learn a true work ethic.

Why is that? It is because, in a very basic sense, work gets meaning from being useful to others. People work in order to provide a benefit. Sure, work may also be fun. We all hope to find work that benefits others while also exercising our talents and giving us pleasure. But many times what others need is not so much fun. That is even more the case when someone has no skills to offer others. In those circumstances, the best he may be able to do is to help pick up dirty towels.

As a result, work becomes more fulfilling the more skills and abilities we bring to bear in helping others. Developing such skills takes time. It also usually takes struggles, setbacks, and maybe even failures. Young people need the chance to struggle so that

they develop skills that are truly their own. Persevering in difficult work also teaches well-earned self-respect. And working
through difficulties also helps people discover what they truly
enjoy. Meaning can come from *any* kind of work (even menial
work). It does not depend on the work being of some special or
transcendent quality. Sadly, children who have the means to jump
from one interest to another looking for meaningful or passionate
work often never find it.

This fact also highlights the difference between work and
education. Even if they do not like it all the time, most children
know that education is for their own good. But as mentioned
previously, a core element of work is that it provides goods for
others. As a result, taking work seriously also involves figuring out
how to make the work, work for you, which is not so much of a
problem in education. Children whose only experience of "work"
is in the midst of student-centered classrooms may resent working for the sake of others. And when they have to do so, they
may have a hard time figuring out how to take care of themselves
while also taking care of others. It is no surprise that people who
have had to work often prove sharper negotiators than people
who may have had better educations but who have never had to
make their work truly work for them.

What then is a parent with wealth to do? One thing is to give
the gift of work, real work. Mike, for example, gave his children
jobs—warehouse jobs, not desk jobs—in his business at an early
age. These jobs gave them a sense of accomplishment and taught
them to find worth even in menial tasks done well. In particular,
their jobs taught them that the value of work comes from providing a useful service for others, even if just sweeping the floor. In
a way, these jobs began to teach his future recipients to look on
themselves as givers.

Another thing prospective givers can do is to ask themselves,
Have my would-be recipients found not necessarily the right job

or their true calling but rather their own ability to make their work, work for them? If recipients are still developing that ability, now may not be the time to give them money directly. Instead, the best gifts for them may be internships or new work experiences. If they have found their ability to thrive in their work—whatever it may be—then financial gifts will likely help them pursue that activity rather than distract them from it. For what they have found belongs truly to them rather than to a job, career, or the money or prizes that flow from work. A significant gift will always be like a meteor. The question is whether it knocks the recipient out of her orbit or brightens the sky.

Not Yet

Determining how much progress recipients have made in this journey is not an easy task. Who could have predicted that Prince Hal, who spent his youth carousing with Falstaff, would become the King Henry V who defeated the flower of French nobility at Agincourt? Certainly not his exasperated father—and likely not even Prince Hal himself.

Serious conversations between givers and recipients over time deepen each other's understanding. Helpful questions include, What are your dreams? To what work are you most drawn? What do you need? How can I help you? Sometimes it helps just to pose the questions and let the other party think about them without feeling required to answer right away.

These conversations can have surprising results. In Chapter 2, we mentioned the example of the son who thanked his mother for a $13,000 gift but added that he didn't want it. He wanted to make it on his own. In another case, a highly successful father wanted to give his son a gift of a trust with several million dollars in it. The son had recently started out in his own legal career. The money could possibly have made a big difference in his standard of living. This father trusted his son and saw that his son had developed his own ability to work. He told his son of his desire to make the gift, but he also asked his son for his thoughts and feelings. The son thanked his father for his generosity and acknowledged the difference that the money could make. But he also expressed his dream of pursuing his calling, for the time being, using only his own resources. He said that he was not sure whether he could effectively fit the additional gift into that dream. He thanked his father, but said, quite sincerely, "Not yet, please."

This was a special son and a special father: Each spoke honestly and the other truly listened. Still, we suspect that if givers and recipients had more of these conversations, we would more often hear "not yet" spoken by givers or recipients. It is not a denial or a rejection. Rather, it respectfully protects the would-be recipient's true wealth: his dream and his work. It gives time, one of the greatest gifts of all.

Whether spoken by the would-be giver or recipient, this "not yet" also protects against an outcome that we see too often in families with wealth: the burden of unneeded riches. We have met many heirs, often first-born sons, who have made it their work to steward the family's wealth. These people are conscientious, hard workers. They preserve their family's wealth but often at the expense of discovering or pursuing their own dreams. They need to ask themselves, "Am I preserving the dream of a past generation, or am I allowing these resources to help me and my loved ones pursue our dreams in the present?" If the former is the case, then the recipient is laboring under the burden of resources that do not promote growth for anyone at present. Givers often worry that their gifts will be wasted on frivolities. Just as bad is wasting recipients' time and efforts tending a fortune rather than building a life.

To be clear, it is not bad in itself for givers to want recipients to undertake the stewardship of their (the givers') dream (see Figure 4.1). The problems arise when givers and recipients do not communicate about which vision informs a gift or inheritance and the consequences for living that flow from these choices.

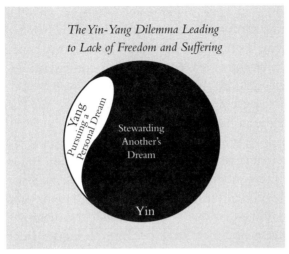

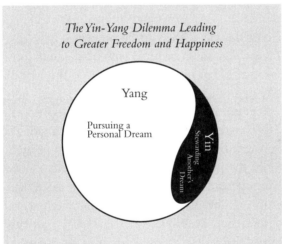

Figure 4.1 Stewarding a Dream

Meteors and Resilience

As we have seen, the image of the meteor is a powerful one for understanding the true power of a gift. Unpacking it a bit more can help us see the wisdom of saying, "Not yet."

Every one of us lives in our own atmosphere, as it were, which forms a boundary between us and the rest of the world.

If that boundary were impermeable, then we would live without learning, cut off from communicating with, helping, or being
helped by each other. On the other hand, if that boundary were
completely porous, then everything around us would affect us.
The result would be that every new impression would wipe out
those that came before. Devoid of atmosphere, for example, the
face of the moon has been largely blasted flat.

The task of growing comes down to navigating that boundary between ourselves and the world, to adaptation and integration.
The same is true for recipients with regard to gifts. If the meteoric
gift comes without spirit, education, and preparation—that is, if it is
really a transfer rather than a gift—it will either destroy the recipient's psychic environment or disintegrate on impact. In neither case
will it produce growth and enhancement. Likewise, if the recipient
lacks the resilience to adapt to and integrate the gift's spirit, either
the recipient or the gift is likely to disintegrate.

Mindful giving, then, requires multiple conditions. The gift
must possess spirit. That requires reflection on the part of the giver,
as we encourage in Figures 4.2 and 4.3.

As the diagrams indicate, spend a moment asking yourself, what
was in my first meteor? That is, what was the content, the spirit, of
the first major gift that you gave to your children or grandchildren?
Then consider the present: What is in your meteor now? Is it fear
or guilt? Is it hope and dreams? Is it something more than money?

In addition to the giver's clarity, the recipient requires preparation and resilience. Resilience is the capacity to bounce back
from whatever the world throws our way. Resilience allows the
recipient's boundary to admit new experiences without too much
rigidity or too much porousness. That is why resilience is a key
variable in determining whether recipients will grow or suffer as
a result of sending gifts their way.

What does resilience involve? Certainly a good physical and
mental state and a strong, supportive social network help. But
most important is the recipient's mental attitude. The experience
of adaptation helps us adapt: someone who has integrated such

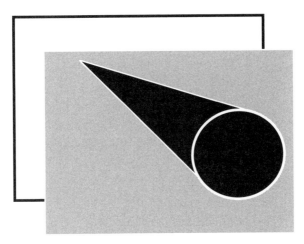

Figure 4.2 What Was in Your First Meteor?

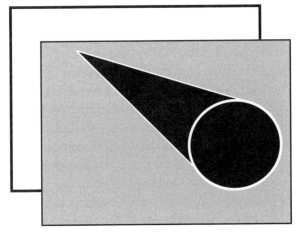

Figure 4.3 What Is in Your Meteor Now?

meteors in the past knows that she can do so again. This is what is known as self-efficacy, the settled assurance that one can integrate such gifts well. Just as important to a positive mental attitude and resilience is what we call the four Cs: control (rather than powerlessness), commitment (rather than alienation), challenge (rather than threat), and community (rather than isolation) (see Table 4.1).

Table 4.1 The Four Cs

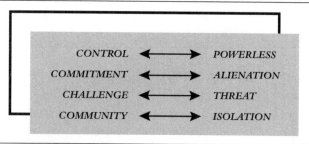

SOURCE: With acknowledgment to Salvatore Maddi, Suzanne Kobasa, and Dennis Jaffe.

When a recipient feels in control or at least a partner in the process of the gift, committed to the good that can come from receiving the gift, emotionally connected to the giver, and challenged to do the best that he can as a recipient of this gift, the stage is set for successful integration of the gift into life. For example, one young man we knew truly took to heart that his grandfather was paying for his college tuition. Rather than partying or feeling guilty about getting something that many of his peers did not, he took this gift as a motivation to make the most out of his college education. Each semester he would share the results with his grandfather, not just for his approval but also to talk about what he was learning. As this grandfather did, mindful givers will help prepare for such success by communicating with recipients as well as giving them opportunities to practice integrating smaller gifts into their lives. As ironic as it may sound, good habits are a key to freedom.

Investing in Recipients

Communication, then, is crucial to a recipient's resilience, adaptation, and growth. Before such communication comes empathy, as we saw in the case of Mike's realization that he, too, was a recipient. There also comes understanding of the stages of life and the stages of giving of both the giver and the recipient. And perhaps the most important step in preparation is that recipients come to know themselves and give to others through the experience of work.

When it comes to the communication itself, how can mindful givers start to foster a sense of choice, optimism, and resilience in themselves and recipients? People often hesitate to talk about money with family members. But sometimes waiting too long is just as bad. One father and son we know had danced around the topic for years when the father's illness prompted a full and frank discussion of his estate plans. When they were done, the son asked, "Why didn't you tell me this before?" The father responded, "Well, you never asked." Neither felt able to start the conversation.

A conversation between giver and recipient does not need to go right into the details of plans. Long before plans are worked out, such conversations should serve primarily as a means for understanding. To that end, we recommend that parents ask their children this powerful question: "How can I use my resources to invest in your dreams?"

With this question, the parents ask the children how to create a relationship, involving wealth, that truly enhances growth—growth of parents as givers and children as recipients. Recall Mike, the father with whom we began this chapter: He felt he was making a bad investment in his estate planning. This question prepares the way for maximizing that investment.

It is not an easy question to ask or to answer. It requires preparation and deep thought. Think of this book as a path of preparation, so that you and your family can entertain this question with the greatest likelihood of it leading to a rich and ongoing conversation.

Questions:
For givers, how can you invest in your recipients' dreams?
For recipients, how can those who wish to give to you invest in your dreams?

Note

1. Jean-Jacques Rousseau, *Emile, or On Education*, trans. Allan Bloom (New York: Basic Books, 1979), 52.

Chapter 5

Spouses

Many people think of giving as a binary affair, involving a giver and a recipient. But in families, much giving comes not from a single giver but from giver*s*, especially a husband and wife.

What follows are our thoughts, based on many experiences, about how to talk with your spouse about giving to family members. This process begins with self-reflection and self-knowledge, the mindfulness that underlies all productive communication. We also offer special considerations for couples who have blended their families or who are facing the prospect of prenuptial conversations (either for themselves or for their children). We suggest as well some thoughts about managing the dynamics of a relationship in which partners bring unequal resources.

Learning from Yourselves and Each Other

To engage your spouse in a successful conversation about giving, it helps first to do some work yourself. In Chapter 3, we offered

47

some questions to help givers go deeply into their own thoughts and feelings about giving. Use these questions or other reflections to examine your wishes and dreams. Encourage your spouse to do likewise. Then talk with each other. Listen carefully to what the other has to say about the outcomes of those reflections. The goal is not to say exactly the same things but to better understand who each of you is and what is most important to each of you.

One couple we met felt stymied at this initial stage of the process. Something was holding them back from having a productive conversation. With some encouragement, they began to talk and to listen to each other. What they learned was that the husband, a successful executive, was afraid to give any money away. Despite their significant wealth, he worried that he and his wife would end up not having enough for themselves. They also learned that the wife was yearning to give and to experience the joy of giving during her lifetime. They were not in agreement about giving. But they began to develop empathy for each other. As irrational as his concerns regarding not having enough money seemed to her, she came to understand his anxiety and accept his need not to give too much financially. Likewise, he came to appreciate her generosity and to trust her judgment. As a result, the husband began to discern ways that he could give to their children and others that did not involve money but rather made use of his considerable business talents. And the wife began to make discerning gifts to family members and charitable groups in amounts they both felt comfortable with. Both were able to transition to the next stage of their lives, focused on generativity, one giving of his talents and the other giving of her financial resources. Both are experiencing the joy of giving appropriate to the challenges and possibilities inherent in their stage of life.

Three-Step Process

With this understanding of each other and this empathic stance, a couple can talk about their shared vision for giving within their family and, just as importantly, begin a conversation with their children about that vision. On the basis of his work with dozens of families, our colleague Charles Collier, former senior philanthropic advisor at Harvard University, recommends a three-step approach to these very important conversations.[1]

The first step is a continuation of the conversation with your spouse. This phase of the conversation moves from your individual values and dreams to the options before you as givers: the *how* and the *what* of giving. The goal here is to get clear about what you think a gift or inheritance should achieve and about how large it should be. You may not agree on all points. The key is to identify your differences, discuss them, and respect them. You may find that there are differences where you thought there were none and points of agreement that you did not expect to find. For this conversation, consider such questions as, What principles guide our decisions regarding our gifts to our children? What are our hopes for future generations? and What amount of inheritance would enhance (rather than subsidize) our children's lives?

The second step shifts the focus from you as a couple to your children. The goal is to listen. Listening does not commit you to a do as your children wish. As we often tell parents, to discuss is not to delegate. As listeners, tell your children that although you retain the right to make final decisions, you will factor what they have to say into your thinking. You can have this talk with one child at a time or with all the children together. A few questions may help you begin to draw out your children's views: How can we use our resources to invest in your futures? What do you see as the meaning and purpose of an inheritance? How important is it to you to manage your inheritance with your siblings, together, or to do so separately, as individuals?

The third step in the process involves synthesizing your principles (from step one) and your children's input (obtained in step two). The key is to do this together, as a couple. Then, respecting your children's willingness to share their thinking with you, share your thinking back with them. That conversation can include a discussion of the principles that guided your decisions, the general nature of the estate plan, and the amounts that they will receive. Explain how you have integrated some of their ideas into your planning. You can also discuss any next steps.

It takes time and trust to overcome the barriers that our society erects to talking about money, especially with those we love most. (As we mentioned in Chapter 4, Sigmund Freud held that love, work, and money were the three most difficult topics to discuss.) But pursued with care and taken step-by-step, the work can strengthen your bonds as a couple.

Blended Families

Nothing is easy about blending families, and dealing with stepchildren and money is one of the greatest challenges. Our children and our money trigger extremely powerful emotions. To make giving work within this context, we recommend tailoring the three-step process to the contours of a blended family. Using this simple process helps spouses tackle the core issues while also managing their emotions.

Again, start with yourselves as a couple and your principles. In this case, your conversation can focus on such matters as how you feel about sharing some of your wealth with your second spouse and his or her children, what you think such an inheritance is meant to accomplish, and what concerns you have if your children have to wait for an inheritance because of your second marriage. These questions can be very challenging to answer, so try to be patient with yourself and your partner in these conversations.

Then, in the second step, solicit the input of your children and stepchildren. How you do so will depend on your family's dynamics. Some parents invite all the children together in one conversation. Others proceed one child at a time. Still others invite each child to speak with his or her biological parent first and then with the couple together. However you proceed, the goal remains to listen to what the children have to say. Questions that Collier recommends to elicit their thoughts are, What are your expectations for an inheritance? and How do you view the purpose of an inheritance from your stepmom or stepdad?

After becoming clear about your principles and plans as a couple, with input from your children, the goal of the third step is to share your thoughts. Again, how you do so—child by child or as a group—will depend on your family. The key is to make the process affirm them as respected members of the family and you as a loving couple.

Prenuptial Discussions

This three-step approach to family conversations can also help enormously when considering prenuptial arrangements, whether for yourself or for your children. In what follows we will focus on the latter situation, mindful that similar steps can apply to your own prenuptial discussions.

Before returning to the process, it is important to put some facts on the table regarding prenups. Sometimes parents have real reasons for wanting their children to get prenups. A family business or some other legacy asset that helps define the family should not be subject to divorce proceedings. Also, if a child is contemplating a second, third, or fourth marriage, or marriage with someone with a history of issues around trust, then—if the marriage proceeds at all—a prenup is likely in order.

However, these are, we hope, exceptional cases. In many wealthy families, much of the wealth has already been placed in trust before the question of children's marriages arises. Therefore, the child who is going to marry may have little or no property of his own subject to a prenup. Also, when we ask prospective spouses how they would want to allocate property they acquire during marriage, they almost always say, "Fifty-fifty." That also happens to be the law in most states.

So, if in many families the wealth falls outside the realm of a prenup, and state law and basic fairness will deal with most property acquired during the marriage, why do most children from families of wealth go through the painful prenuptial process? The answer is can often be summed up in one word: fear. Some of that fear may be their own: They may fear that divorce without a prenup will be longer and uglier than one with a prenup. But most prospective spouses are hopeful, not fearful. The fear usually comes from parents and grandparents. And fearful parents and grandparents are often the ones with the power to demand that young people get a prenup.

The key is to clarify, in your heart, what emotions are motivating the prenup. A prenup is often a meteor—though not a giving one. It may fly out of nowhere into the middle of a budding relationship. It may cause a massive impact, especially if it is full of fear.

Being honest if this fear is the motivator is the start to handling prenups well. One more consideration is crucial. Many parents forget, when urging a prenup, that to make it effective the law requires full disclosure of each party's financial interests to the other and the other's counsel. This disclosure means that the parents of the prospective spouse must share *their* balance sheet, as it affects their child, with the potential in-law—and with their own child. We have seen many occasions when this was the first time when the child herself learned the full scope of the family's wealth. In such cases, the prenup meteor gets bigger and bigger and potentially more disruptive.

How then should parents—since they are usually the ones behind the prenup—handle this meteor? The first step is for parents and, separately, the child (and prospective spouse, if he is present) to become clear about their principles. Think of yourself as giving them (and yourself) the gift of becoming clear about what really matters to them (and to you) regarding money and marriage. Topics for each parent to think through include what you think the prenuptial arrangement is meant to accomplish, why you do (or do not) want a prenup, and what you worry will happen if you or your child do (or do not) have a prenup. For parents, in particular, it is helpful to ask yourself what it will take to bring your children into this conversation, whether or not you could let your child make her own decision about a prenuptial arrangement, and, very important, in what ways you want to share some of your wealth with your daughter- or son-in-law.

The second step in the process brings the parties together to listen and learn from each other. It may work best for you to meet as a couple with your child first, then subsequently with your child and her prospective spouse together. Or you may want to meet as a group. If your children are not yet at the stage of considering marriage, but you want to prompt their thinking, you may wish to meet with all your adolescent or adult children together to hear their thoughts.

When you meet with your children, you will want to understand what they see as the purpose of an inheritance, why a prenuptial arrangement is important to them (or not), and whether they believe they can maintain separate financial resources and still have a viable marriage. As always, it is important to listen for the principles that underlie their various viewpoints. Finally, ask them what dreams they have for the future of their relationships and families.

Parents have the prerogative to shape their estate planning more or less as they wish. They do not have the prerogative to dictate their children's prenuptial arrangements, which must be entered freely. So the third step in this process involves bringing parents and children back together for a follow-up conversation to the second step. This conversation likely involves sharing what you believe you heard from each other and what conclusions you have come to on that basis. It can also move on to action steps to take based on those decisions. If the decision is to have a prenup, then the ground has been laid for all parties—including the prospective spouse—to understand the principles for the decision and to view the process as the entrance to a thoughtful family's life rather than as a bar against full inclusion. The goal is to remove the fear from that meteor and replace it with wise decisions based on love, understanding, and ultimately freedom.

Fiscal Unequals

Before concluding this chapter on spouses and family giving, we want to spend a moment on the dynamics that arise in a partnership of fiscal unequals. You may have heard the variant on the Golden Rule: He (or she!) who has the gold rules. It is not a recipe for domestic happiness. Demographics and changes in the role of women in society also mean that more and more women bring greater resources to relationships. Because they sometimes challenge prevailing norms, such relationships require great forethought, communication, and compassion.

The key to success within fiscally unequal relationships is acknowledgement. Acknowledge the nature of your financial relationship, recognize its profound effect, and positively accept the likelihood that it will continue throughout the relationship. Likewise, it is important for your families to acknowledge this reality and both accept and honor it.[2]

How can you get closer to such acknowledgement, if you are in or are considering a relationship of fiscal inequality? It is critical for each partner in the relationship to consider, and then to discuss as a couple, core questions about the role of money in your lives and in the relationship. For example, Susan Piver[3] offers a host of such questions, including,

- What values—including about money—did I inherit from my family of origin?
- What role does money play in my life?
- Do I want us to keep our money separate or mingle it together?
- What are my ambitions? Am I satisfied with my ambitions? Am I satisfied with my partner's ambitions?
- Where will we live?
- What happens when one of us wants to stop working?

The key to this process is not that you expect to arrive at the same answers to these questions. Most couples differ on significant points. The real goal is to come to a place of understanding of the other's personal beliefs and to empathize with each other. This empathy and understanding will only add to your intimacy and your conscious ability to manage your differences. After all, the differences will make themselves felt, one way or another. Thoughtful attention to these questions and honest conversations about them will help you make the most of your similarities and differences.

So much of the time we think about giving in vertical terms, flowing from grandparents or parents on high down to children or grandchildren below. As important as these vertical relationships are, the horizontal ones—of spouses or partners—are crucial, too. Arguably, the largest gifts, most often repeated, take place between couples rather than between parents and children. And if the spirit of the gift does not energize these horizontal relationships, it will likely not infuse the vertical ones. To make sure that does not happen, give yourself and your spouse, or your prospective spouse, the greatest gift: the gift of listening with a truly open heart.

Questions:
What do you know about your spouse's views of wealth, gifts, or inheritances? What would you most like to learn?

Notes

1. Charles Collier, "Financial Inheritance as a Family Conversation," July 2011. Copies are available from Harvard University, Office of Development.

2. James E. Hughes, Joanie Bronfman, and Jacqueline Merrill, "Reflections on Fiscal Unequals," 10–11. This paper is available at www.jamesehughes.com.

3. See Susan Piver, *The Hard Questions: One Hundred Essential Questions to Ask before Saying "I Do"* (New York: Tarcher/Putnam, 2002).

Chapter 6

Grandparents

We initially framed the subject of family giving as part of the broader topic of parenting. Parenting, after all, is largely a form of giving. And giving brings us face-to-face with the core challenge of parenting: How do we enhance rather than subsidize our children's lives even as we let them (and ourselves) grow into free, independent, and flourishing individuals?

But parents are not the only givers in a family. After all, in many cases, they may not have as much to give (at least financially) as their own parents do. We want to consider grandparents, too, both because they have a different relationship to their grandchildren than the children's parents do and because they are in a different position in their own lives with respect to giving and receiving.

Grandparents' Great Opportunity

Grandparents have an opportunity for a special connection with their grandchildren. They and their grandchildren often enjoy a love that is not as complicated as the love between parents and children. Grandparents can give love without feeling obliged to focus on discipline. They are also usually less distracted by the demands of business. What's more, the kinds of regrets so often felt with respect to their own children are less likely to get in the way of their feelings for their grandchildren. Grandchildren, in turn, can look to grandparents as unstinting sources of love and affirmation rather than as authorities against whose will they must one day test themselves.

Grandparents are often in a different position with respect to family giving than parents are. By virtue of their age and reduced needs, some grandparents have more wealth (in terms of money, time, and experience) to give. As the contemplation of mortality becomes more real and perhaps more bearable, they also have the incentive to initiate plans and to make gifts.

Typically, grandparents have completed the first stage of life, of receiving, and the second stage, of building and achieving their own dreams. They have entered the third stage, of giving back and supporting others. Though they may retain their own strongly held views, they may also be better able to objectively discern the effects their choices have on the future.

For example, one grandfather we met was determined to keep the government from getting any of his hard-earned wealth. He was equally determined to tell his children, from beyond the grave, how to spend the money he left them. But when we asked him what effect he wanted his wealth to have on his grandchildren, he stopped issuing pronouncements and started thinking. His grandchildren, he reasoned, "were not fully formed yet." Therefore, his choices could make a real difference to the kinds of adults they became. He turned to the serious consideration of what to do, not just what to avoid.

Involving Parents

If you are a grandparent, the opportunity you have—as well as the great consequences of your decisions—makes it crucial to approach family giving mindfully. In some ways, your giving is more complicated than that of your grandchildren's parents. Giving as a grandparent means starting *not* with thinking about the ultimate recipients (your grandchildren) but with thinking about the people in between: your children and their spouses. For many of us, this step can prove a real stumbling block. It is only natural to have mixed feelings about your children: Often they are the source of our greatest joys and our greatest pain. You may also not entirely approve of how your children or their spouses are raising your grandchildren. You may have concerns about involving your children's spouses in discussions about your wealth. And every grandparent's greatest fear is doing or saying something that will cause your children or their spouses to limit your access to your grandchildren. All these feelings, which are quite common, can cause grandparents to hesitate to talk openly with their children and their spouses about their plan to give to their grandchildren. Acknowledging these feelings and the reasons behind them is an important first step. At the same time, as understandable as this hesitation is, it can cause a missed opportunity.

The conversation between you and your grandchildren's parents can be quite powerful and beneficial. For example, we worked for many years with a wise grandfather, whom we will call Frank. Frank's parents had created a flourishing business that generated great wealth for them and their seven children. His parents put most of the wealth from the business into trusts benefiting Frank and his siblings. Through much of his life, the business was not worth much. But as Frank aged into his seventies, the business took off and the trusts were eventually worth well into the nine figures.

When we met Frank, he was thinking about his estate planning. By then, though divorced, he had 3 adult children and 10 young grandchildren. He had to decide what would happen to the assets in his trusts, some of which were set up to skip his children and benefit his grandchildren. When we asked him about his wishes, he said he had formulated an initial plan. The most important thing, he said, was promoting independence. We observed, though, that while he valued independence, his existing plan would affect the lives of his grandchildren without giving his children any say in the matter. Once the contradiction was presented to him, he immediately recognized it.

As a result, Frank undertook a journey of discernment. He worked with us to prepare for conversations with each of his adult children and their spouses, to share with each one the choices he had before him, and to solicit their input on the effects they would like the trusts to have on their children. He asked his adult children when and how they, as parents, would want the money to proceed to the beneficiaries. He invited input on each grandchild, to better shape his gifts. He made clear that he retained the prerogative to give as he chose, but he listened and he incorporated much of his children's thinking into his eventual plan. He then shared that plan with his children as a group, so that they could see the ways he used their ideas and how, as a result, some gifts to their children would differ from others.

Frank's example teaches some important lessons to grand-parents considering giving. First, communication with parents is essential. Frank children had good relationships with him, though they had their moments. They had little preparation, however, for the discussion of his wealth, so these conversations were eye-openers to them. Because of the business' rapid growth, they had not seen that meteor coming. They deeply appreciated his seeking their input on the possible impact on their children.

Second, the process of inclusion does not mean grandparents give up control. Frank was a smart and determined man. He knew what he did and did not want to do. His children's input informed him without determining his choices. As we have said, to discuss is not to delegate.

Third, grandparents, just as any givers, need to think about who the recipients are. You may know your grandchildren well but likely not as well as their parents do. Seeking parents' input is crucial to giving successfully.

Clearly, grandparents show their respect for their children as parents by communicating with them about their plans for giving. Mutual respect is the key to making these gifts successful. By enhancing communication and respect, the process can be a gift to the whole family.

Grandparents and Philanthropy

Frank and his children already had a good basis for communication when it came time for him to discuss with them his trusts and their likely effects. But perhaps you see the need to rebuild communication with your children. In that case, coming to know your grandchildren—as a precursor to giving wisely—may require more than a conversation with their parents.[1]

One way to do so is to engage with your grandchildren in a process of giving together via philanthropy. This process gives you a chance to interact directly with your grandchildren in a serious endeavor. It also gives the younger generation a clear role in the family's management of its wealth. Such a role may be important as grandparents begin to relinquish active management and hand over more of those duties to their adult children. As nascent elders, grandparents still have much vitality and wisdom to share. Philanthropic activity with grandchildren gives the older generation a forum to teach and to learn.

Philanthropy, in and of itself, is a practical teaching tool: virtues are learned through the process of giving to others. It offers grandparents a chance to take a role in teaching grandchildren the values of gratitude and stewardship. It also gives your grand-children a powerful way to work together to shape the family's impact on others.

How might this philanthropy work? First, consider including all grandchildren age six and over. In some families, grandchildren may be more than 20 years apart in age. Despite this difference, we find there can be a shared experience among the grandchil-dren in their love and admiration for their grandparents, creating a bond that overcomes the gap. In addition, in families with trusts, frequently the grandchildren form a class of beneficiaries regard-less of age. As a class, all the grandchildren share the same financial interests in the trusts. This similarity of financial position fre-quently leads to a need for the older grandchildren to mentor and lead the younger. Shared philanthropy helps build a foundation for such a relationship.

Second, think small in terms of size of grants, since a wide age range means that even grants of $100 to $500 will seem large to the younger children.

Ways to Give
A *private foundation* is controlled by a private group of trustees and directors and usually makes grants to nonprofits (known as *public charities*) performing services or producing goods for others (e.g., a museum or a hospital). A *donor-advised fund* is a fund set up at a financial institution or community founda-tion allowing the donor or donors to make grants to public charities. A donor-advised fund receives more favorable tax treatment than a private foundation. Either a private founda-tion or a donor-advised fund may be known as a *philanthropic fund*. A *grant committee* oversees grants from either type of entity. The committee requests, reviews, decides upon, and tracks grant requests.

Third, use the simplest structure possible for making these philanthropic grants. If you already have a private foundation, set aside a small portion of the capital specifically for that purpose. If such a vehicle does not exist, a donor-advised fund can likely be arranged for amounts of $10,000 or more.

Fourth, let grandchildren 12 and older form an investment and administrative committee for the philanthropic fund. Although most people readily see the benefits that come from philanthropy in terms of learning to give, they often fail to appreciate that a private foundation or philanthropic fund is a business and can provide an educational setting for acquiring needed investment and administrative skills that are immediately transferable to the family's for-profit activities. Give the investment and administrative responsibilities to the older grandchildren as early as possible. You can act as mentors and advisors to your grandchildren in this function, retaining ultimate decision-making authority until you are confident of your grandchildren's capabilities.

Fifth, develop a clear process for how the grant committee will request and vote on grants. Most children six or older are capable of proposing and advocating a grant request. The older the grandchild, the more written material regarding the grant recipient can be required. When grandchildren are 10 or older, they may want to make site visits to the location of the proposed grantee or, if impossible, speak with the director of the proposed recipient organization. It may be best for the oldest grandchildren to be asked to put their skin in the game by somehow actively participating in the organization to which their requested grant will be made.

Even relatively young grandchildren can devote serious thought to this process. We know a six-year-old child who had proposed a grant to a local animal shelter. The next year, she and her grandparents visited the shelter to see how they were doing. She left concerned that the animals were not being cared for in the ways she imagined they would. As a result, she sought a different recipient for her grant dollars that year.

Although the written material, site visits, or participation are all important, the key step in the grant-request process is the oral presentation by the requesting grandchild, which takes place at the annual meeting of the grandchild-grandparent philanthropic fund. At this meeting, let each grandchild present a grant request. Following the presentation, you and the other grandchildren, with great care and affection, critique the request and vote on the application. What could be more fun than to sit with one's grandchildren and discuss their passions and discover who they are? From the grandchildren's perspective, the process offers an opportunity to receive your wisdom and hear about their own siblings and cousins' passions.

Finally, it is important that the parents of the grandchildren stand apart from this process as much as possible. This exclusion is not an unfriendly act. To the contrary, for this process of intergenerational giving and sharing to work, parents will want to actively promote the direct interaction of the two generations. In doing so, they will quickly understand that their intervention would only inhibit that interaction. Some parents may doubt the benefit of this intergenerational practice because their relationship to their own parents has been unsatisfying or even broken. In such cases, the grandparent-grandchild fund should wait until the relationship between grandparent and adult child is more fully restored.

Establishing a grandparent-grandchild philanthropic fund of this sort offers numerous benefits. For grandchildren, it helps develop crucial life skills. When grandchildren come forward and make their grant requests, they are learning public speaking and leadership as well as how to advocate and ask for something on behalf of others. We encounter so many clients who tell us how much they wish they had learned as young people how to overcome their anxieties about speaking and standing up for what they believe. They wish they had learned early on to come confidently into a room of people and ask for what they want, to prepare an agenda or a proposal, and to advocate for a position in which they passionately believe. The added benefit of grandchild-grandparent philanthropy is that in making and advocating grant requests, all of these skills are brought into play in a loving, caring atmosphere toward an outcome that benefits others rather than oneself. The families we know who have adopted this practice understand that if their young members are to be ready to take on leadership roles in or outside the family, these are critical skills to learn.

As a result, grandparent-grandchild philanthropy also contributes to sound family governance. It prepares grandchildren for leadership and teaches them the values of the family and to care for others. It offers grandparents an active role in family governance so that their wisdom and their love and affection for their grandchildren can be fully engaged. For both the grandparent and grandchild, it offers a shared experience, a chance to learn about each other as they are discovering the world and its needs through giving wisely.

Despite how easy it is today to travel and connect via technology, the modern world is not an easy place in which to be a grandparent. In the past, many grandparents and grandchildren lived together in the same house or on the same city block. Today, the two generations may go for months without seeing each other, connecting only for a holiday or an occasional weekend. Yet if you are a grandparent, you have so much to give. And most grandparents would give almost anything to learn about and connect with their grandchildren, either by talking openly with their adult children about their grandchildren or by sharing philanthropic activities with them. In the end, these activities serve two ends: They help grandparents give wisely, and they serve as a precious gift to all—grandparents, parents, and grandchildren.

Questions:
For grandparents, what do you think are the best ways you can promote your grandchildren's growth and flourishing?
For parents, what are the ways you think your parents can best promote your children's growth and flourishing?

Note

1. For more on this topic, see James E. Hughes, *Family Wealth: Keeping It in the Family* (New York: Bloomberg Press, 2004), Chapter 12.

Chapter 7

Trustees

M any times family leaders ask us, "Whom should I choose as a trustee for my family's trusts?" The choice is a critical one. As we will discuss more in Chapter 11, family trusts can have an immense impact—positive or negative—on a family's long-term flourishing. As the overseer of those entities— and a crucial link in the cycle of the gift—good trustee(s) can make all the difference.

The Choice of Trustee

As important as the choice of trustee is, proceeding in a mindful way requires stepping back and considering some preliminary questions. The first is not Whom should be chosen? but rather Who is doing the choosing?

Perhaps your initial reaction to the question of who will choose the trustee is, "Well, I will, of course!" This natural reaction points squarely at the complexity of the trust relationship. The creator of the trust, the grantor, often makes the initial selection of a trustee. He will also likely determine, in the trust document, the method for selecting successor trustees. Sometimes the existing trustees choose their own successors. Sometimes a trust protector may have the power to step in and remove and appoint new trustees. Increasingly, beneficiaries are being given the power to appoint new trustees—and, at times, remove existing ones.

Trusts 101

A *grantor* or *trust creator* establishes a trust by placing assets in it, to be governed by a legal document known as the *trust document* or *trust agreement*. A *trustee* takes legal title of those assets, overseeing their care and disbursement in line with the trust document and state law. A *beneficiary* is the person or class of people who benefit from the assets in the trust, in whichever ways the trust document specifies. Sometimes grantors establish *trust protectors* who have the power, in special circumstances, to remove or appoint trustees or to amend the trust document. A *successor trustee* takes the place of a trustee who resigns or is removed.

Clearly, selecting a trustee is not like picking out a car or a house for your own use. The very term *trustee* implies a relationship of trust with one person (the grantor) for the sake of another (the beneficiary). The grantor makes the initial choice, particularly if the beneficiary is young or not yet born. But as the beneficiary ages and matures, it becomes more and more likely and reasonable that he or she will and should have a choice in who serves as trustee. Indeed, one of the main goals for a trustee is to help a beneficiary achieve the maturity to make such choices wisely.

The Type of Trustee

Given that goal, we encourage grantors—and later beneficiaries—to consider first and foremost the type of trustee needed and the qualities that trustee will need. Most people tend to personalize these decisions; that is, they naturally think first about who might be right for the role. My brother? My business partner? My corporate attorney? That is not necessarily the best place to start. A mindful approach combines thinking about the type of trustee, the qualities of the right trustee, and, above all, the desired relationship between the trustee and the beneficiary.

There are many types of trustees. Individual trustees are people who take on the responsibility of overseeing the management and distribution of trust assets. The individual can be a professional—such as an attorney or accountant—or a nonprofessional whom you trust, such as a family member or friend. Institutional trustees are corporations that serve in the same capacity, usually trust companies or banks with trust charters. They perform this work as a business function, using committees and well-considered procedures to manage and disburse funds.

Whether an individual or institutional trustee makes the most sense—or some combination of the two—depends on the circumstances of your family and the trust. Your choice will involve considerations of control, the complexity of the assets, the length of time of the trust, and expenses.

The Relationship between Beneficiary and Trustee

These are important considerations, but they are secondary to the main goal: finding a trustee who will help beneficiaries mature and thereby use the gift of the trust to enhance rather than merely to subsidize beneficiaries' lives. You want a trustee who will not only facilitate your gift but make a gift of her own, namely, the gift of helping the beneficiary become a free, independent, mature individual. Such a trustee, who gives the gift of freedom to beneficiaries, will allow you to feel free, too, as you make the gift in trust.

Too often, the trust relationship encourages dependency rather than independence. Parents worry about this outcome. And the sad effects are not lost on beneficiaries. We have spoken to hundreds of beneficiaries over the years. We sometimes ask them, "On the whole, has your trust had a positive or a negative impact on your lives?" Over 80 percent of beneficiaries respond that the overall effect has been negative. Some benefit!

Again, the trustee can make all the difference in this outcome. The core question is what relationship the trustee will have with the beneficiary. As we show in Figures 7.1, 7.2, and 7.3, in most

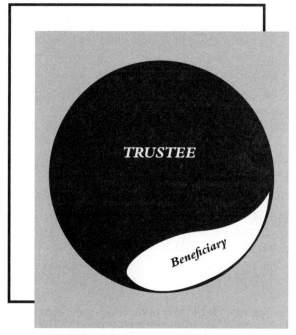

Figure 7.1 The Trustee–Beneficiary Relationship, Trustee Dominant

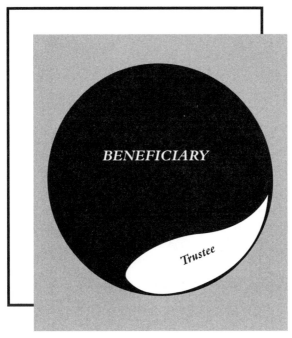

Figure 7.2 The Trustee-Beneficiary Relationship, Beneficiary Dominant

trusts, the trustee holds a dominant position. The beneficiary makes requests; the trustee decides and disposes. The bigger the trustee gets, the smaller the beneficiary becomes. In other cases, the trustee just rubber-stamps the beneficiary's request, in effect turning the trust into a piggy bank that subsidizes rather than enhances the beneficiary's life. In contrast, we recommend that, as beneficiaries mature, the trustee and the beneficiary become more like equal partners, ensuring that the gift in trust truly promotes the beneficiary's life and growth.

How can you lay the foundations for such a relationship? Start by looking for a trustee who can, to use political terms, serve as a sort of regent. Remember, in the early stages of the trust's life, the trustee will likely be acting for the good of a beneficiary who is not yet mature or able to make his own choices.

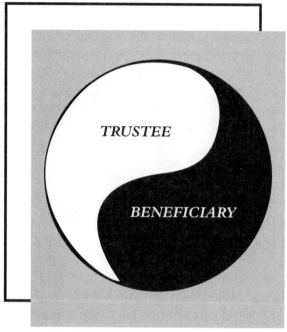

Figure 7.3   The Trustee-Beneficiary Relationship, Balanced

Doing that well requires a special set of characteristics and skills. As Jay Hughes and Patricia Angus explain,[1] this trustee as regent

- Remembers that her ownership of the trust property is only temporary.
- Knows how to relinquish power and eventually transition it to the rightful beneficiaries.
- Focuses on the education of the beneficiaries in order to prepare them for ultimate ownership of or control over the property.
- Maintains open and honest age-appropriate communication with the beneficiaries.
- Is responsible to all beneficiaries, present and future, in accord with the trust provisions.

- Subordinates his interests to those of the beneficiaries.
- Possesses the necessary skills to do this work well.
- Earns her authority rather than taking it for granted.

Good trustee-regents provide excellent administration and prudent investment of the trust assets.[2] But beyond service to the trust assets, the trustee as giver will educate beneficiaries about the trust, its provisions and powers, its assets and the work of investing, and about the financial world that the trustee and beneficiary inhabit. That way the beneficiary will be in a better position to understand and evaluate the trustee's work and make wise choices regarding the trust and his own life.

Beyond serving as a prudent investor and an educator, in the regency, a trustee can help beneficiaries by serving as a mentor.[3] Mentorship is a demanding but deeply rewarding relationship. It partakes of something divine. After all, the original Mentor, who appeared in Homer's *Odyssey*, was actually Athena, the goddess of wisdom, in disguise. A mentor helps someone undertake the multistage journey to maturity. That journey may involve further education, travel, or inner exploration. It may involve a sort of coaching as the beneficiary faces important choices about school, career, and family life. The existence of mentors reflects the reality that life's journey involves transitions and that we all do better when someone caring—somewhat at a distance, sometimes even in disguise—offers us advice and counsel along the way.

Over time, of course, a trustee's role as mentor will diminish as the beneficiary completes her odyssey and finds a true home in personal exploration, work, and family. At that point, the trustee becomes more the beneficiary's partner and representative. Going back to our diagrams about the trustee-beneficiary relationship, the trustee moves to a more equal place. To act as representative of a mature, well-educated, and mindful beneficiary is a role any trustee can be proud of.

A Regenerative Role

A good trustee plays a special role within a family's cycle of the gift. The trustee is, after all, the legal recipient of a grantor's gift. But the trustee holds that gift for the sake of another, the beneficiary. In this simple but profound way, a giving trustee models for the beneficiaries the centerpiece of the cycle of the gift: viewing oneself as a recipient who gives to others and so keeps the spirit of the gift alive.

In that respect, a good trustee's role is not so much generative as regenerative. The grantor generates the gift, often at that third, generative stage of life. The real challenge for the family then begins: Does the gift become a subsidy, which contributes ultimately to entropy and decline? Or does the gift continually enhance the family's life? A trustee can play a crucial part in making sure the gift is regenerative—that is, it retains spirit—rather than entropic. He does so by first playing the role of regent and then, later, of mentor and then partner. The trustee also can do so by reminding beneficiaries and other family members of the reasons for the gift. Too many trustees succumb to a faceless, administrative role. In truth, a regenerative trustee may embody the cycle of the gift more powerfully than any other member of the family.[4]

Questions:

For trustees, what are the most important steps you can take to promote beneficiaries' growth?

For trust creators, what criteria will you use to select a trustee?

Notes

1. James E. Hughes, *Family Wealth: Keeping It in the Family* (New York: Bloomberg Press, 2004), 189–194.

2. The prudent investor rules that originally governed trustees' work as investors derive from a famous Massachusetts case in 1830, *Harvard College v. Amory*, in which the Supreme Judicial Court required that trustees "observe how men of prudence, discretion, and intelligence manage their own affairs, not in regard to speculation but in regard to the permanent disposition of their funds" (26 Mass. 461). Even as regards the limited subject of investing, and in 1830, we see here the insistence that trustees not rule over trusts from the confines of their own castles but rather get out into the world and observe what others are doing. It is a good moral for beneficiaries, too.

3. See a fuller discussion of trustees as mentors in Hughes, *Family Wealth*, 181–188.

4. For a fictional example of a trustee who worked with a grandparent to establish a regenerative gift, see Jim Stovall, *The Ultimate Gift* (New York: David C. Cook, 2001). The story was later turned into a feature film of the same name.

Chapter 8

Elders

M any people play an important part in family giving—spouses, grandparents, trustees—but from the family's perspective, few roles are more crucial or more complicated than that of the family elders. In Shakespeare's *Richard II*, "old John of Gaunt, time-honored Lancaster," sought to give advice to his nephew King Richard. Instead, when he died, his wealth became "the ripest fruit" to fall into Richard's reckless hands.

As Gaunt's failure reveals, elders are not just olders. Grandparents, for example, may become elders: they may become a persuasive voice for deliberation and integrity in the family. But to do so takes more than getting older; it takes a variety of qualities and actions. Likewise, Gaunt's fate points to the tension in the role of elders. Let's consider that tension and, more important, the qualities of true elders and the great gifts that they can bring to their families.

Intergenerational Dynamics

Increasing longevity and growing wealth have only intensified the issue that faced King Richard and his uncle. The following dynamic is quite common: If you are an older parent, the current first generation, you may wish to enjoy your elder years in peace and give decision-making authority to your adult children. At the same time, you probably want to continue sharing with your children the best advice you can offer. Likewise, if you are an adult child, you probably want to give your parents respect and receive their wisdom. Yet you also most likely want the authority to make decisions, without the older generation pulling the proverbial rug out from under you.

Most families let this tension play itself out covertly in one decision after another. Sometimes the first generation may call the shots, with grudging acceptance from the second. Other times the second generation may pursue its own path, wishing that the first was more clearly on board. Obstructing the needed conversation is fear: namely, the parents' fear that they will be pushed aside and the adult children's fear that their decisions will be vetoed. Fear reflects a breakdown of giving: each side fears that its gifts (of authority, advice, and respect) will not truly be given or received. The tragedy of this situation is that each generation's gifts leave them feeling more constrained rather than freer.

To get at the heart of this dynamic, two questions are crucial:

1. What is the appropriate role for the family to give the senior generation?
2. How can the senior generation remain active in the family's affairs in ways that are appropriate to their seniority but allow their children a chance to grow and lead?

The first question focuses on form: What are the particular roles, activities, or positions that senior members of the family should engage in or hold? The second focuses on function and spiritual consequences, both for the senior generation and for their adult children. Most important, these questions prompt conversation within and between the generations about the gifts that each has to offer the other.

Growing Elders

Wise elders can be a wonderful gift to a family. What can you do if you want to serve this role—or help someone else in your family do so? As mentioned, elders are not just olders. Age is not the sole criterion for your becoming an elder. Many families find the notion of cultivating elders attractive but also feel stymied about how to prepare their members to become elders.

Elders are not made; they grow. Such growth naturally involves moving through the cycles of individual development and family life, including the experience of being a recipient, being a giver, giving back, and ultimately receiving again. Everything you experience and learn throughout your lifetime contributes to your becoming an elder.

There are also specific areas of learning or practice that are essential to the role of elder. Many families believe that the focus of wealth education should be on the young. But, given their stage of life, young people are often more inclined to put their energies into finding their own way and becoming their own persons rather than immersing themselves in the details of their families' affairs. Ironically, it is more often the family's elders who can benefit most from education.

What is it that elders should learn or practice? First, practice developing comfort in not knowing. As seductive as it is to claim to know it all, if you are an elder, you will gladly echo the motto of investor and philanthropist Sir John Templeton: "How little we know." An elder is the opposite of an expert, not in the sense of being ignorant, but rather in being open to learning and treasuring questions over answers.

Learning to listen is also a key. When we work with families on the work of growing elders, we share with them concepts that are core to cognitive-behavioral psychology, which teaches that our actions and emotions are based on certain thoughts or scripts in our head and that these automatic thoughts are themselves based on deeply held beliefs. In other words, what we believe leads to our thoughts, which in turn drive our actions and feelings (see Figure 8.1).

Most of the time, people operate at the surface level of actions, emotions, and thoughts. But as an elder, you will listen for the beliefs that lie beneath. By understanding and surfacing your own and other family members' beliefs, you can influence, strengthen, or challenge the resulting thoughts, feelings, and actions. This work gives shape to elders' particular ability to lead from behind.

The ability to surface your own and others' beliefs connects with another of elders' core capacities: You become the home, as it were, for *discernment* in the family. Discernment is the process of connecting a rich sense of the human good with the particular

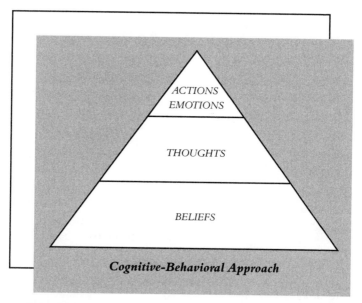

Figure 8.1   The Cognitive-Behavioral Triangle.

choices and actions before us. It has two requirements: The first is to obtain and continually refine a vision of the good in all its complexity; the other is to figure out the choices and the steps that can lead from where we are to some eventual approximation of that good.

No one is born able to discern well. That is because it takes time and experience to develop a rich sense of what is good for yourself and others. Doing so effectively usually takes quite a few hard knocks and disappointments. Also, it takes time and experience to gain the practical know-how that allows you to see how choice A connects with choice B and possibility C. These are all matters of lived experience. That is why discernment is also sometimes called "practical wisdom."[1]

If you are becoming an elder, then you have had experience in practical affairs and have lived long enough to develop a rich sense of the human good. Combined with an ability to listen to others and to their own hearts, your discernment will powerfully enrich family deliberations.

Lastly, if you are becoming an elder, you embody two other characteristics: patience and play. You know how to conserve your voice, thereby making your words all the more powerful. As an elder, your place is not in the day-to-day decisions of the family. The more you get into the weeds, the more you diminish your own authority. Elders also have a sense of the playfulness, creativity, and spontaneity that are part of shared family life. Patience and play are not easy lessons to learn (or relearn). Most of our lives we are told to get serious and get things done. Many people take their productivity and multitasking as a badge of honor. One of the greatest challenges of age and retirement is to step back from such busyness and honor the more reflective, relational, and playful aspects of life.

The Work of Elders

These are some of the characteristics embodied in successful elders, but if you are an elder, what is it that you end up doing within your family? What, in particular, are the gifts you bring?

Each family will come up with its own answer to this question. However, we have seen some patterns, both in history and in practice, that indicate several possible roles for successful elders:

- To tell the family's stories.
- To remind family leaders to follow the family's agreed-upon rules and to reflect the family's values and goals in the process of governance.
- To effectively mediate internal family disputes.
- To conduct the family's rituals.

As an elder, your stories give the family a crucial gift: a sense of being distinct from any other family. This sense is crucial if family members are to feel committed to the family's present and long-term success. A sense of distinction provides a powerful framework for decisions. If your family has a clear idea of its lineage, it will engage naturally in the seven-generation thinking popularized by the Iroquois saying "It should be our hope that the care and thoughtfulness we bring to our decision making today will be remembered and honored by our descendants seven generations from now, just as we honor those who seven generations ago made it possible for us to be here today." Your family is also more likely to take the approach that both Alexander the Great and Julius Caesar took to their planning: *speude bradios* or *festinate lente*, Greek and Latin, respectively, for "hasten slowly." By themselves, these sayings are just words; framed by family stories, lineage, and a sense of distinction, they acquire great power.

The effects of the elders' retelling of family stories brings us to the second gift that elders within your family can offer: to remind family leaders of the family's agreed-upon rules, values, and goals. Put simply, as an elder, you keep the rest of the family honest. Families often fall into habitual patterns and let important insights or practices languish. Elders, with their experience, serve as the family's memory, keeping past agreements and decisions alive. Sometimes just asking family leaders open-ended questions is enough to get the family as a whole to connect their values with their choices.

The third gift that elders offer to families is to mediate family disputes. Whether in ancient tribes or in modern industrialized societies, human beings look to their elder statesmen to mediate conflict. Usually these elders help the parties take the dispute out of the frame of established alliances or legalistic processes so that matters can be tackled more informally and directly. Playing such a role effectively requires scrupulous attention to boundaries, confidentiality, and trust. Age helps because it brings with it greater experience in the world and the ability to remind conflicting parties to look to the big picture, the issues that really matter. It takes a special elder—and a special family—to allow for this sort of mediation.

The fourth gift that elders bring is to conduct the family's rituals. Examples of elders giving this gift include Virgil in Dante's *Divine Comedy* (conducting Dante through the dark wood of despair), Athena in Homer's *Odyssey* (conducting young Telemachus on his journey to manhood), and the rabbi in a bar or bat mitzvah. Why are elders so important to ritual? Rituals combine play and seriousness, freedom and control, which we will consider in more detail in Chapter 12, where we discuss rituals as a form of gift. Even in secular settings—such as, for example, the swearing in of a governor or president—ceremony brings together the human and the divine. As such, rituals require not just administration but also ordination. They require someone who engenders respect—the authority that goes beyond a vote or a title—to conduct them.

These four tasks—telling stories, reminding family leaders of the family's values, mediating disputes, and conducting rituals—are the great gifts that elders bring to family life. These tasks also make elders vital to the cycle of family giving. If you are an elder, you receive the family's care and respect. You give back, from your experience and wisdom. And you are a gift yourself. The ancient Greeks and Romans described their elders as "treasures in the house,"[2] whom they compared to statues of the gods. The hero Aeneas, the founder of Rome, carried only two things away from

his home in Troy when it was sacked by the Greeks: the icons of
his household gods and his elderly father, Anchises. The conjunc-
tion of the two was not accidental.

The elders within a family may not yet be suited to these
four tasks. And many families do not have their own elders. As
a result, we have often seen people from outside the family step
in to bring to the family some of the gifts of elders. These out-
siders may be longtime family friends. Very often they are trusted
advisors from legal, financial, or human services professions who
know the family members well. An elder does not need to be a
biological member of the tribe. If your family has not yet grown
its own elders, you may very well want to have these external
elders working with you until a true elder emerges from your
family members. If you have not already, we encourage you to
seek out them and their gifts.

Question:
Who are or have been the wise elders in your life, and why
do you consider them as elders?

Notes

1. See Barry Schwartz and Kenneth Sharpe, *Practical Wisdom: The Right Way
   to Do the Right Thing* (New York: Penguin, 2010) as well as Paul Schervish
   and Keith Whitaker, *Wealth and the Will of God* (Bloomington: Indiana
   University Press, 2010).

2. See Numa Denis Fustel de Coulanges, *The Ancient City* (Baltimore,
   MD: Johns Hopkins University Press, 1980).

THE HOW OF GIVING

Chapter 9

Control versus Freedom

In the preceding chapters you have met some of the people who are part of the process of family giving. Now let's turn to the various *ways* of giving and the *types* of gifts. Our focus remains on how a discerning or mindful approach may enhance a giver's and a recipient's growth rather than subsidize existing forms of behavior and contribute ultimately to entropy and decline.

The Myth of the Free Gift

While speaking once to an audience of individuals with wealth about the spirit of the gift, we described how spirit naturally creates a cycle in giving, one in which givers feel an obligation to give and recipients feel the duty to receive and give back or give forward. At that point, a young woman raised her hand. "Aren't gifts supposed to be free?" she asked. "If you get a gift, shouldn't you be free to do—or not do—whatever you want with it?"

She had a point. Most people would probably agree that a gift is not truly a gift if it comes with strings attached. In many countries, the law reflects this sentiment. For example, if you make a gift but keep tight control over how it is used, your gift may not be complete for tax purposes. In this respect, the law encourages givers who set their gifts—and their recipients—free.

That said, many would-be givers have very definite views on how they want recipients to use their gifts. As one grandfather told us candidly, "My children tell me that my dead hand's going to try to control them from the grave. And I tell 'em they're right!" In many countries, the laws regulating gifts and trusts allow givers to exercise such control. Laws, after all, are no more consistent than the human soul from which they spring.

It seems, then, that no gift that is truly a gift, and not merely a transfer, is completely free. At the same time, if the gift comes with no freedom at all, it is not a gift. Balancing control and freedom is core to giving wisely, and we encourage you to take, once again, a mindful approach, beginning with reflecting on yourself and your would-be recipients. Do not focus only on control or freedom but instead ask yourself, To what degree, with this gift, have I used my control to give my recipients—and myself—the freedom to grow?

Cui Bono?

How can you begin this process of discernment? When considering the possible restrictions or controls you may place on a gift, ask yourself, *Cui bono?*—To whom is the benefit?

For example, we knew an aging executive who had developed a very elaborate estate plan. His main goal, he stated quite proudly, was to make sure the government got not a dime of his hard-earned wealth. He had little interest in charity, so most of his wealth would proceed in trust to his descendants. But he had also imposed numerous restrictions on his children's ability to access these funds after he was gone.

We asked him to explain the principles behind these choices. He began enumerating the follies, as he saw them, of the government. He also sadly described the follies, as he saw them, of his children. Then we asked whom the plan would benefit and how. Here he was less certain. "*I* am sure," he said, "that *I* don't want to see *my* money going to waste and abuse." Though it was hard for him to see it, his plan was very *I* focused.

As an executive, this man knew how to direct an organization to achieve results. His control served a clear end. But the real beneficiary of his estate plan remained himself. He could rest satisfied that, as much as possible, he had devised a plan that would not contribute to what he saw as waste and abuse. Only when we brought up his grandchildren, who were still quite young, did he begin to be able to step away from his own good—his pride in protecting his money—and think more concretely about the good of others. His concern for his grandchildren allowed him to step from unreflective to mindful giving.

Perhaps you are like this executive: Control may be part of your character. It is neither good nor bad. Control contributes to great success in some areas of life and creates great difficulties in others. For many of us, the desire for control strengthens when it comes to wealth we have created ourselves; we identify so closely with the wealth that it becomes part of us. This desire tends to increase with age, as we react to losing control in some parts of life by seeking greater control in others. If you are a parent, the desire to take control of your children's affairs flows almost seamlessly from your desire to care for and protect them. If you are an adult child, you are likely seeking greater control over yourself and your affairs.

All these expressions of control are natural, and they often serve good purposes. The task is to be mindful of this desire and to ask honestly, Who benefits? My recipients? Me? Or both of us?

The Giving of Accounts

To get a deeper perspective on the subject of control, compare, for a moment, common current practices around family giving with practices that were more common in years past.

Good Exclusions

As we mentioned in Chapter 1, the *annual exclusion* allows a person to give up to a certain amount—currently $13,000— per year to anyone else free of any gift tax. Such gifts may be made outright or in trust and may take the form of cash, securities, debt-forgiveness, life insurance premiums, and so on.

If you have followed a fairly standard estate plan today, you may have given gifts to your children and grandchildren throughout their lives. You have probably taken advantage of the annual exclusion to give cash, securities, or real estate. Perhaps you have made these gifts in trust or in other ways that restrict the recipients' access to the assets. Some gifts you may have made outright and with no restrictions. You may be like many givers we meet today, who say that they would not feel right telling their children or grandchildren what to do with the $13,000 or the condominium they helped them purchase. But when it comes to gifts after death, many of these same givers often establish elaborate estate plans that tie up the money in trust and impose various restrictions or incentives on it.

This practice differs markedly from some of the practices once used by the wealthy. George Peabody, for example, was one of the first great American investment bankers. By the middle of the nineteenth century, he had built up a fortune of several million dollars—a huge amount then—by selling American bonds in England. Peabody did not have children of his own. But during his life, he gave quite generously to his siblings, his nephews and nieces, and to a host of charitable causes.[1]

With each of these gifts, Peabody would write a letter, telling the recipient what he expected the money to be used for and asking for a letter in reply that accounted for its use. In many cases, these letters gave rise to a correspondence stretching over years, as his sister or nephew or someone would let Peabody know, down to the penny, how his gifts were used. When he died, however, Peabody left his family members several million dollars in trust, giving them access to the income and some of the principal to benefit from as they wished. With variations of their own, other nineteenth and early-twentieth century magnates such as Cornelius Vanderbilt, Andrew Carnegie, and John D. Rockefeller Sr. pursued a similar approach.

Today, many givers give fairly freely during their lives but more strictly after death, whereas in the past some of the most notable givers required careful accounts from recipients during their lives but gave more freely after death.

What can we learn from these differences? Certainly, the level of control you exert over lifetime gifts or bequests will always depend on who your children or grandchildren are. But we encourage you to consider the wisdom inherent in Peabody's approach. He discerned that during his life he had the greatest gift to offer to his loved ones: the gift of his counsel and advice. He stated his intentions for how his gifts should be used not simply to be controlling but also to help his family members use those gifts wisely. He recognized that a conversation between giver and recipient could benefit both. His recipients learned to state their needs honestly, clearly, and reasonably. And he learned to listen, to empathize with them, and to support their true needs. Rather than veiling gifts in silence or treating them as an unmentionable subsidy, this giving of accounts brought both sides closer together and contributed to the enhancement of their lives.

In his written conversation with his recipients, Peabody was both learning and teaching. By giving Peabody an account of what they wanted and what they did with their gifts, Peabody's family members and friends learned or honed practices of good financial management as well as the virtues of moderation, patience, and self-knowledge. As a result, they were in a much better position to receive wisely and to manage the less-restrictive gifts that he made in his estate plan. Peabody's lifetime practice of conversation with recipients, and teaching them through that conversation, laid a sound foundation for his freer bequests.

Today, you may feel reluctant to inquire too closely into your children's or grandchildren's financial affairs. Parents who have sought to become their children's friends may feel especially hesitant to appear to be telling them what to do. That said, we believe Peabody's example suggests that beginning such a conversation around lifetime gifts can be seen not as telling but rather as teaching and listening. Once recipients receive a true gift, it is their prerogative to do with it what they wish. But that prerogative does not preclude you, as a giver, from sharing your advice beforehand and asking for some account afterward. Doing so may lay the groundwork for making even freer gifts in the future. Good habits, after all, are the key to freedom.

Letting Be

Let's revise, then, our starting point about gifts and freedom. At first glance, people say that gifts should be free. On reflection, we say that gifts should *promote* freedom. The promotion of freedom is compatible with and even requires some degree of control.

As we said, control is not a bad thing. If you have accomplished good things in your life, you probably have done so in part through self-control and self-discipline. If you have led or lead an organization, you need some control to achieve results.

A sense of control is often part of a basic feeling of well-being. No one feels good when feeling powerless or out of control.

The key, then, is not to let the desire for control harm yourself or others. That means, as we have discussed, asking yourself whom your control benefits. It also means being clear about the limits to your control. For all our powers as individuals or as a society, what we cannot control is far greater than what we can. You cannot control what your children do with their lives. You cannot control some of their most important choices, such as those relating to careers or marriages. As we age, we begin to lose more and more control over our own bodies. Almost all of us have the power to cut short our lives. But even the most powerful among us cannot add one extra day to his life span.

The natural human reaction to these uncertainties is fear, and when we feel fear, we often seek control as an antidote. This emotional progression can become a vicious circle, causing us to take rigid stances precisely when we would do best to let go. In response, a core piece of self-knowledge is the recognition that true control comes not from our power over external matters but from within. Our greatest control comes from discerning what we can control and what we cannot control—and trusting our ability to deal with whatever may happen.

Easy to say—but not so easy to do! We have met many parents who are deeply disappointed with the choices that their adult children have made—and yet they still want to give these children some sort of financial gift. At the same time, they do not want those gifts to subsidize further destructive ways of life. Our response has always been, "Get clear about what you really want to do—or not do. Make your plan. Communicate that plan to your children as calmly as possible. And then let go." That last part is probably the hardest.

A story that has been told and retold many times illustrates the wisdom of recognizing the limits on our control and letting go. A poor farmer and his son had one horse that helped them in many of their tasks around the farm. One day the horse ran away, and the son cried, "How terrible! Now we shall starve!" The father said, "Who's to say it's good? Who's to say it's bad?" The next day the horse returned, bringing three wild horses with it. The son rejoiced, "How wonderful! Now we shall be rich!" The father again said, "Who's to say it's good? Who's to say it's bad?" The son tried to break in one of the wild horses. The horse threw him and he broke his leg. Again he wailed, "Oh, father, now I'll be a burden to you!" The father said, "Who's to say it's good? Who's to say it's bad?" The next day the army swept through their village drafting all able-bodied young men to fight at the front. All whom they took were killed, but they left the farmer's son with his broken leg.[2]

The farmer knew that he could not predict the future. He knew the limits of his control. He was willing to let things be. Letting go, letting things be, is profoundly connected to giving and receiving. If you let them be, you give your recipients the opportunity to be who they are, for good or for ill. If you let yourself be, you give yourself the opportunity to be who you are as you age and change. Under the influence of modern technology, so many of us seek to make the world—and each other—conform to the ideas and desires we have in our heads. Letting be reverses this stance and allows us to give ourselves to the world and to receive what the world has to offer.

There is an old debate about whether the human soul is more like a hand, grabbing and giving shape to the world around us, or more like an eye, receiving what the world has to show us.[3] It is not for us to decide where the truth lies, but we certainly believe that the cycle of the gift suggests that our receptivity is one of our greatest powers. It may be that, at our best, we human beings are more receivers than givers. That is perhaps the deepest reason for attending more carefully to the perspective of recipients than many of us normally do. The spirit of the gift that we have talked about may shape us more than we shape it. Moments of receiving that spirit, giving, and letting go of our gifts remind us of these fundamental questions.

From this perspective—recognizing that true control comes from within—we see that control and freedom merge. The two apparent opposites turn out to be one and the same. Your control becomes something good and worthwhile when it lets you and your recipients grow in your freedom. And freedom is truly freedom when it takes shape under self-control—the control that can be taught through caring conversation and good examples. It is the kind of control that ultimately comes not from "a will" but from your own will. It appears not in "a trust" but from trusting yourself. True gifts are those that let both givers and recipients grow in their freedom.

Question:

If you were to write a letter to the recipients of your gifts, what would it say?

Notes

1. For more on Peabody, see Franklin Parker, *George Peabody: A Biography*, rev. ed. (Nashville, TN: Vanderbilt University Press, 1995 [1971]).

2. An ancient form of this story appears in the medieval *Gesta Romanorum*, or *Roman History*, in which an angel instructs a hermit in the mysterious ways of divine Providence.

3. Consider, for instance, the Greek philosopher Aristotle's *On the Soul*, Book 3, Chapters 4–8. For a translation, see Aristotle, *On the Soul and On Memory and Reflection*, trans. Joe Sachs (Santa Fe, NM: Green Lion Press, 2001).

Chapter 10

Fair versus Equal, Separate versus Together

There are some core practices to mindful giving. Among the most important of them are to reflect on yourself, your principles, your values, and your dreams and to try to understand recipients, who they are as individuals as well as their principles, values, and dreams.

But as we have seen, family giving frequently involves a more complex system than the twosome of giver and recipient. Often, there are multiple recipients. If you are a parent or a grandparent, you are probably wondering, "Should I give my children exactly equal amounts?"

The Balancing Act

The common response is, "Treat your children [or grandchildren] fairly but not necessarily equally." Equitable, not equal. Easier said than done! The fair-versus-equal balancing act is a tough one. Closely related to it is another dilemma, the question of whether givers should expect or encourage recipients to enjoy their gifts or inheritances together or separately.

Fairness versus equality is such a hot topic because most of us start with the premise that everyone is equal to everyone else. If you have children, you do not want some of them to feel more or less loved than others. You also know that if your children do not feel that they are loved equally, it will likely lead to resentment and conflict. How many times have we heard that fights about a family business or an inheritance have roots in beliefs about who dad or mom loved best decades before?

But nature and our desires do not always see eye to eye. Children do differ from one another—physically, mentally, and emotionally. Some have more drive; others have better judgment. Siblings raised in the same home environment may develop vastly different characters. Even twins raised together turn out differently.

As a result, if you have children, you know that you must treat each of them differently, not just based on their ages but based on who they are as individuals and what each one needs to flourish. What works for one may not work for another. Treating them the same may hinder rather than help children grow as individuals.

Most of us square the circle of fair versus equal by arguing that while we often must *treat* our children differently we still *love* them all equally. But that distinction seems hard to maintain when it comes to gifts, especially financial ones. Arranging for a tutor only for a child with a reading disability but not for his reading-proficient sister seems fair. But giving a $13,000 annual exclusion gift to the struggling artist but not to her brother, the established investment banker—as fair as it looks—is a choice that would likely make some parents feel uneasy. The net result, in our experience, is that if you plan to treat your children unequally, in your giving or bequests, even if for good reasons, make sure to communicate those reasons early, often, and with great clarity.

The same logic applies to separation and togetherness. Your children's individuality will lead each one to pursue distinct paths in life. What parent has not encouraged his children to "pursue your own dream"? At the same time, most of us long for our families to remain connected and together. Perhaps you also secretly or not-so-secretly harbor the hope that your children will return to a family business or your family neighborhood or city. Wealth can be a powerful solvent, giving individuals the means to live their separate lives. So, too, it can strongly glue family members together through trusts or business interests. To switch metaphors, it turns up the volume on both dilemmas. As one mother put it to us, "Why would I want my gifts to promote freedom, if that freedom leads to my children taking their own separate piles and running off to the four corners of the earth?"

Pot Shots

To approach these dilemmas mindfully, let's consider an example. We met a family several years ago composed of three elderly siblings, their ten adult children and spouses, and their many children. This family had done everything right in their financial and estate planning. Long before they sold their successful high-tech manufacturing business, they transferred many of the shares (at a relatively low value) to a family limited partnership. They then gifted those shares, at a discount, to a family trust. They further discounted the value of those gifts by making them through split-interest vehicles (in this case, charitable lead trusts), which lessen the present value of the gift by assigning some of its value to a charitable recipient. In this case, the charitable recipient was a family foundation, so while giving away some of the money they still retained control over its disbursement.

The ABCs of Estate Planning

Estate planning involves a host of entities with as many acronyms as a federal agency. Here are a few that the reader may find helpful:

- A *family limited partnership* (FLP) allows parents to gift assets to children at a discount while retaining significant control over the assets.
- A *family trust* operates for the benefit of multiple family members and often multiple generations. It is contrasted with a *spousal trust*, which benefits a widow or widower.
- A *charitable lead trust* (CLT) makes payments to charity for a number of years and then leaves the remainder to family members. The charitable gifts discount the value of the eventual gift to family.
- A *charitable remainder trust* (CRT) makes annual payments to a family member and then leaves the remainder to charity. Both CLTs and CRTs are split-interest entities because they benefit both charitable and noncharitable recipients.
- A *family foundation* is a private charitable foundation whose board is controlled by members of the same family.

As a result, when a deal too good to refuse came along to sell their business, they had transferred tens of millions of dollars to their family trust at a tax cost of nearly zero. Their legal bill for this work easily surpassed $100,000, but compared with a possible tax bill 100 times as large, it was a good value. They came to refer to the family trust as the pot. They had put pretty much all their financial wealth into that pot.

By taking these steps, this family made great progress down the path we mentioned at the end of Chapter 3, when we were discussing the "Nothing too much" precept. Rather than dispersing their wealth among individual family members, they collected their financial resources in a trust that was understood by everyone to benefit the whole family. In addition, they pursued wealth education: They put together a formal educational program to teach all adult family members about how the various parts of this mechanism would work. And they established a family governance plan, setting up a number of boards made up of family members to oversee the different parts of the whole and make decisions, such as where to invest, where to give, and how much to distribute. Their planning was reflective and thoughtful.

In short, they accomplished a lot. But after a few years of living with the pot, strains became evident. First, they noticed that much of the income generated in the family trust was being siphoned off for the charitable lead trusts' payments to the family foundation. Such distributions were not burdensome during the heady days of ever-rising markets, but after the financial crisis, they began taking significant bites out of the rest of the pot.

At about the same time, they realized that while they spoke about the pot as belonging to the whole family, including future generations, some members enjoyed its bounty more than others. The elderly siblings, who had spent their whole lives working hard in the business, were taking large distributions from the pot in order to maintain their lifestyle. None of the adult children begrudged their parents their luxuries, but as the market declined and the spending continued, some family members began to wonder whether the pot would be there for future generations.

In addition to concerns about the long-term viability of the pot, the family also began to face challenges regarding the day-to-day use of the funds. Because the family members did not retain much in the way of assets for their personal use, they needed help from the pot when they wanted to make major expenditures (such as for a house, car, or tuition). This created tension, since 13 households spread around the country naturally had different tastes and needs.

Our point in sharing this story is not to criticize this family. As we mentioned, they accomplished a great deal—in planning, wealth education, and governance—and they made significant strides toward their goal of growing long-term family wealth. But their very progress reveals the challenges inherent in the task of family giving.

Flourishing

Why did this family, who had done so much right, still find it so difficult to talk about fairness versus equality, separateness versus togetherness? Part of the problem was their focus on the forms or structures in which their giving took place. This focus led them away from thinking about the functions, or purposes, these structures served.

Another part of the problem was that they focused too much on how much: How much were the charitable trusts getting? How much was each family member getting? How much would be there in the future? From the point of view of how much, equality and togetherness tend to rule. As a result, family members got stuck arguing about making equal disbursements for even relatively minor expenditures (such as for iPhones or computers) in order to ensure that everyone got the same amounts. They needed a richer vision of the human good than how much.

Our response in working with this family was to shift the frame of the debate from how much or togetherness—the quantities and structures—to the qualitative goal: enhancing their family's life rather than subsidizing a certain lifestyle. Changing that frame was the starting point for resolving their dilemmas.

What do we mean when we talk about flourishing? In Chapter 1, we shared our view that families flourish when they help each generation—parents, children, and grandchildren—live their lives, on their own and together, as flourishing individuals. To make this point more concrete, in working with many families, we have identified three major elements of family flourishing. These include a *sense of lineage*, the *experience of joy and fulfillment*, and a *focus on future growth*. These three elements reflect the reality that families are always in a process of growing from the past, in the present, toward the future.

Lineage is a family's ability to celebrate a sense of who they are in the light of where they have come from. You may be cultivating lineage already without knowing it, by articulating your family's core values, sharing family history and family stories, and sustaining certain traditions and rituals. You can also develop your family's lineage through philanthropy, choices of where to live, and attention to your family's reputation in the community.

You cultivate present joy and fulfillment whenever you engage in direct, honest, and timely communication; respect family members' need for separateness and togetherness; and help your family focus on their strengths. Like individuals, families often spend much of their time focused on what happened in the past or worrying about what will happen in the future. A serious and loving attention to present joy is crucial for true flourishing.

You focus on your family's future growth when you encourage parents to be both teachers and learners. You can also do so by cultivating a sense of purpose in individual family members and by helping each one build skills and knowledge with a view toward his or her independence and personal flourishing.

With the family with the pot, we did not discuss in depth all the elements and activities proper to family flourishing. Instead, we focused on those areas where they felt they had work to do. They had a strong sense of lineage. And they had a clear commitment to future growth. But in their attempts to cultivate present joy and fulfillment, they were challenged.

Promises

As mentioned, the first step for this family was to change the frame of their discussions from subsidizing a certain lifestyle to enhancing family flourishing. By making that change, they began to defang the tough conversations they were having about fair versus equal, separate versus together. This change also helped them think creatively about how to manage their differences.

They observed that they really did want to do what was best for their family. But they also wanted to enjoy their own lives as individuals. In fact, they felt sure that one of their greatest strengths as a family was their shared belief that their commitment to each other justified their hope of enjoying individual happiness.

What a wonderful belief! So we asked them how they might demonstrate that commitment. We helped them come up with a promise, made to each of them by the others: "I will help you in your own journey of happiness, and I hope that you will help me in mine."

This promise has proven extremely powerful, both in this family and in many others. It is a promise that prompts a question: How can I help you? And from that question arises a discussion. Just think about having such a discussion in your family. What forms of help, in the next year or two, would allow you to fulfill your promise to them? And what forms of help would allow them to fulfill their promise to you? Having this discussion every couple of years can have a tremendously positive effect. If you do so, it will help all family members see that your family is truly something more—in a qualitative rather than quantitative sense—than the sum of its members or the aggregate of its possessions.

In the case of the family with the pot, the more they became convinced that what really mattered was their individual and shared present joy and fulfillment, and that each of them had something important to contribute to that flourishing, the less important it was that each of them received equal financial value from the pot. They even came to justify unequal distributions and some separation on the basis of their shared promise to enhance each other's lives rather than to subsidize a common lifestyle. After all, since they were all different individuals, such enhancement would naturally take different forms. One grandchild was best helped by going to a private school with a visual arts program. Another did better going to a public school that supported his special needs. Their richer vision of the human good allowed them to develop and tolerate varied practices.

As a result of this work, the family also came to agree that individual households should have some assets of their own, so that they did not have to rely solely on the pot. To that end, they decided that individual households should be expected to work and keep the products of their separate labors. In addition, they distributed some assets directly from the pot to each household. They followed the maxim of "Nothing too much" in doing so, but they distributed enough so that—combined with the expectation for continued work—it was unlikely that people would have to come back to the pot any time soon. They also terminated the charitable trusts that were devouring the pot's liquidity. They did so at some tax cost, because they saw that they would live with less anxiety and less conflict if the pot's income was not disappearing so rapidly. Paying some tax is not always bad, they concluded. Finally, they established clearer and agreed-upon guidelines for making future distributions, especially for older members of the family who would not be expected to work to maintain their lifestyles.

Such steps take time and many discussions, perhaps heated ones. But if you pursue them, they will increase respect among the individual members of your family. The key to success in this approach is for members of your family to hold two core commitments: to your family as something more than the individuals and to each other's personal quests for happiness. For the family with the pot, a shared promise and a focus on flourishing served as a bridge to practices that encouraged enhancement and growth rather than subsidy and entropy. They can do the same for other families, too.

Questions:
How can you help other members of your family in their personal quests for happiness?
How can they help you?

Chapter 11

Giving Outright, via Loans, or in Trust?

If you have thought this far about how to give well to family members, you have probably come up against the big question: What about gifts in trust? There is no more commonly recommended way of giving large amounts than through trusts. "Don't put your trust in money," goes the old saying, "but put your money in trust." And there is probably no way of giving that causes parents and grandparents more worries than trusts. *Trust babies* or *trustafarians* are just two common nightmares. Rather than promote freedom, gifts in trust can make givers feel locked into a plan they come to regret and can make recipients feel locked out of enjoying the gift as responsible adults. *Trust* means anything but, say some beneficiaries. How, then, can one balance gifts of trust and outright gifts so as to enhance independence and growth rather than to subsidize entitlement and dependency?

Options

As you probably know, in an outright gift, the recipient takes full control and ownership of the gift (usually cash or securities). In a gift in trust, the property is held in trust for the recipient's benefit but is not usually under the recipient's control. In addition, families often use loans in both these cases to accelerate the amount of property they can give. For example, rather than giving an adult child $13,000 over 20 years to buy a $260,000 condominium, a parent would likely *loan* the child $260,000 today to buy the condo and then *give* the child the principal of the loan over 20 years. That way the recipient owns the property—and any future appreciation of the property—from the start. A giver can set up the same sort of loan to a trust for someone else's benefit.

As always, each of these ways of giving has its pros and cons. Some families we know have creatively combined these ways of giving into something they call a family bank. It is a powerful model that we will look at more closely in a moment. First, let's take up each way of giving on its own.

Sharing the Spirit

If you have started giving to family members, you have probably made some outright gifts. They are the simplest way to give. The benefit of such gifts is their immediacy. If your son is at college and you pay the tuition bill, he can keep going to class. If you give your daughter 100 shares of IBM stock, she will get the next dividend check and she has the immediate right to sell those shares and use the proceeds as she wishes. For someone who has a present need, outright gifts make a lot of sense.

This immediacy also is the source of the major drawback of outright gifts: They are difficult to infuse with spirit. The most immediately usable property—cash or publicly traded securities—has little life of its own. It does not easily carry much spirit, the way a family home or a piece of personal jewelry might. Also, such gifts tend to be easy and sometimes even invisible to giver and recipient. But an invisible gift is likely to end up as a transfer.

To infuse such gifts with spirit, slow them down and give the spirit a voice. Discuss an outright gift before you make it. Have a conversation with the recipient about the ways that the gift may help him. See if there are ways to help beyond the financial. Add a note or some other personal touch to express your wishes. If you are the recipient, reply with a note or some other expression of thanks. Even the simplest outright gift can be a moment for ritual that adds to its spirit.

Making Loans Work

As mentioned, you can use loans to accelerate the amount of your gifts and to make sure recipients benefit from any appreciation in the acquired property. Just as business loans can leverage returns, so too gift loans can leverage the financial results of giving. Prudent businesspeople use leverage with care. So do wise families.

The challenge with gift loans is that they can be even more invisible than outright gifts. Take the example of loaning your child the money to buy a condominium and then giving away that loan through annual amortization of the principal. On the face of it, you bought your son or daughter a condo—a very generous gift. But unless you are very attentive, neither you nor your child will likely take much notice of the underlying loan and its amortization. The legal gift is invisible.

As a result, gift loans pose two main dangers. First, they easily obliterate the spirit of the gift. After all, if the condo is not really a gift but the product of a loan, neither you nor your child is likely to feel much like a giver or a recipient, generous or grateful. The annual debit from the amortization table is the real gift. And it is pretty hard to feel generous or grateful about an accounting notation.

Second, because they are so invisible, gift loans may undermine your recipients' understanding of credit. In the real world, the principal balance for a loan does not simply disappear. Also, the interest rate on family loans is usually set very low, to increase the financial benefits of the gift. Market rates are likely much higher. For these reasons, if you make such loans to your children, you may be hindering them from becoming prepared to deal with getting and paying for more conventional credits, such as bank mortgages or car loans. Perhaps billionaire investor Warren Buffett did his daughter a favor when, after she asked him to loan her some money to renovate her kitchen, he replied, "Go to the bank and do it like everyone else."[1] Habit is the basis of freedom. Gift loans can undermine good credit habits.

In light of these challenges, use gift loans sparingly and with caution. If such a loan is called for, then structure it as closely as possible to a commercial transaction. Discuss with your recipient why a loan makes sense. Clarify what property will stand as surety for the loan. Do not reflexively set the interest rate as low as possible: come up with a rate that makes sense based on the recipient's means. Most important, clarify the purpose of the loan and make that the object of your generosity and your recipient's thanks. In these ways, you can safeguard the spirit of the true gift as well as help prepare your children or grandchildren for dealing with nonfamily lenders. You will be freeing yourself—as a generous and wise parent or grandparent—and you will be helping them become more independent.

Why Trusts?

Legally, trust documents are hard to follow. But morally, they are simple: They spring from care. You care for a beneficiary. To express that care, you give property to someone trusted—a trustee—to use that property in order to take care of the beneficiary.

That is the idea, anyway. In reality, something else usually happens. To allow the trustee to care for the beneficiary, a trust separates ownership from the enjoyment of property. The trustee owns the property but does not enjoy it. The beneficiary enjoys it but does not own it. As a result, trusts also offer significant tax benefits, protection of assets from lawsuits and accidents, and control over the management of assets. Though the main purpose of trusts is to care for people, in most cases the secondary purposes—all of which concern property—take over and become the real focus.[2]

We have already mentioned that trusts can have bad effects on beneficiaries, which can also cause givers to suffer grantor's remorse. But they can have good results, too. They make sense if you want to keep wealth within your family but also give "nothing too much" to any one family member. Likewise, if you (or your recipient) say "not yet" to a possible gift, you may find a trust a prudent holding vehicle. And gifts to unborn descendants will occur before you can know who the beneficiaries are. In such cases, you have to delegate the process of judgment to someone else, namely, a trustee.

So how can you make gifts in trust that retain and preserve spirit and freedom? It is not easy to do. The main challenge is not to succumb to the temptation that trusts often awaken: the urge to combine the desire for dynasty with the desire for personal control.

Giving Forever

As a reminder, a *grantor* is the person who creates a trust by giving assets to it for the benefit of someone else. A *perpetual trust* (also known as a *dynasty trust*) is one with no termination date specified by the trust document or state law. It envisions benefiting members of its class of beneficiaries (usually descendants of the grantor) forever. Until recently, most states outlawed perpetual trusts by a law known as the Rule against Perpetuities. In the last decade, this rule has been abolished in many jurisdictions.

Family trusts have long been associated with dynastic, old money families. But perpetual trusts are no longer just for the significantly wealthy. Many legal and financial advisors encourage clients to set up trusts envisioned to last for 999 years or more. States in North America, the Caribbean, and Europe have changed their rules regulating trusts to allow for longer trust terms and greater control by grantors over trusts in order to support this dynastic dream. With the trend toward loosening estate and gift taxes, it has become possible for thousands of families to put billions of dollars of assets into perpetual trusts.[3]

Perpetual trusts have their uses. They can save families enormous money in taxes and allow for consolidated family control over important assets. At the same time, the more you seek to control the future use and enjoyment of a trust, the more that trust may cost your family in human terms. In our experience, during the first generation of a family's wealth creation, most assets remain under the ownership and control of the wealth creator. Upon the transition of assets from the first to the second generation, we find that it is typical for at least half the assets to enter into perpetual trusts, with trustees who are not family members. When we work with families of the third generation and beyond, it is not unusual to find that more than 90 percent of the assets are held in trust. We describe this movement as a trust wave that washes assets away from family members and into trust.

This wave can leave money protected and human beings stranded. On the basis of data from more than 3,000 wealthy families, researchers Roy Williams and Vic Preisser found that more than 90 percent of families had lost their family wealth—meaning that they no longer had any meaningful control over it—by the third generation.[4] These negative outcomes are not just statistics. If your descendants see money as locked up in trust, they are less likely to inquire into its purposes and its management. They are more likely to see it as a source of unearned income, leading perhaps to dependency. Or they may see it as unneeded riches warping their choices about work or living.

Our goal is not to criticize families who become swamped by the trust wave. Rather, we hope to encourage you to reflect before creating such vehicles. Who would your perpetual trust benefit? Is it for the recipients or for your own ego? Further, is it likely to work? Is it reasonable to expect that the trust will continue to operate as planned two centuries—or even two decades—from its inception? Consider the message of Shelley's sonnet "Ozymandias":

> I met a traveller from an antique land
> Who said: "Two vast and trunkless legs of stone
> Stand in the desert. Near them on the sand,
> Half sunk, a shattered visage lies, whose frown
> And wrinkled lip and sneer of cold command
> Tell that its sculptor well those passions read
> Which yet survive, stamped on these lifeless things,
> The hand that mocked them and the heart that fed.
> And on the pedestal these words appear:
> 'My name is Ozymandias, King of Kings:
> Look on my works, ye mighty, and despair!'
> Nothing beside remains. Round the decay
> Of that colossal wreck, boundless and bare,
> The lone and level sands stretch far away."

All that said, trusts do have a place in a plan for family wealth.[5] To see that place better, let's consider a family who managed to combine these ways of giving—outright, via loans, and in trust— with a true orientation toward enhancement rather than subsidy.

The Family Bank

The father of this family was a practicing attorney, who served as trusted counsel to many of the largest global companies of his time. But he was as comfortable with the work of Marcus Aurelius, the Roman emperor and philosopher, as he was with

114

THE HOW OF GIVING

legal briefs. His highest praise was that a man or woman's choice
or action was "sound."

He had four children. A few weeks after the youngest of these
had graduated college, he called his eldest child, a son (and also an
attorney), into his office. He announced that with the completion
of the siblings' collegiate careers, he had decided that they, as a
family, were to create a bank. His son naturally asked what in the
world this meant. His father replied, "It's really quite simple."

He went on to explain to his son, and eventually to his other
children as well, that he and their mother had decided that they had
more than enough money to live comfortably. "Nothing too much"
was a precept he knew well. With due allowance for their personal
needs, the mother and father had decided to dedicate their remaining assets to a family bank. This bank would take the form of various
family trusts, educational accounts, and other savings vehicles.

The purpose of the family bank, he explained, would be to support
the children and eventual grandchildren and great-grandchildren in
their own personal pursuit of happiness. To do so, he asked the children to serve as the board of the bank. They would have discretion
over disbursements. He and their mother would be happy to provide
asked-for consultation, but they would hold no veto. Eventually the
children could nominate their successors to the board.

Disbursements could take the form of loans, secured against
property or unsecured. Or they could take the form of grants,
requiring no repayment. As the family practiced with the bank, they
decided that any disbursements for the acquisition of property—
such as for the down payment on a house—should be made as
loans and repaid. But disbursements made to help a family member
through hard times should likely be a grant.

The family's experience with the bank was not always smooth.
The father and mother found it hard at times to resist the urge
to suggest certain disbursements or to question others. Two of the
siblings went through difficult divorces requiring significant grants
from the family bank. One sibling died in an accident, requiring

the remaining siblings and the bank to take more responsibility for his surviving spouse and children. The siblings also pursued their own careers, which earned some of them much more income than others. As a result, loans and grants from the bank to the various siblings and their children were not equal. But their shared spirit of helping each other grow allowed the bank and the family to grow even in the face of such inequality.

An enormous spirit infused this gift of the family bank. It has inspired the lives of these family members and many others who have come to know them. It was, in the patriarch's word, sound.

Form versus Function

We can take a number of lessons from this patriarch and his family. First, their process of discernment began with a vision of family wealth as separate and distinct from individual family members' resources. As a result, they took concrete steps to distinguish the family's resources—the family bank—from the individuals'.

Second, this family made full use of their options for giving, through trusts, loans, and outright grants. But they maintained a loose structure amid these options. The function of the family bank was clear: to foster the pursuit of happiness of individual family members, present and future. The form was more free-flowing. Form follows function, not the other way around.

Third, unlike many givers who proudly create complex (and expensive) estate plans, this patriarch deliberately understated his plan's complexity. He kept the family focused on the simple purpose of the bank, because that is what is most important, rather than any complexity, which turns out to be only a nuisance. His quiet pride rested in the lives he enhanced, not in the plans he could have paid for.

This observation leads to one last point. Because he was a lawyer trained in a traditional understanding of the law as a profession, this patriarch felt comfortable avoiding legalese. He wanted to be free from running the show. And he wanted his children to be free to make responsible choices on their own. He did not want a legal structure forcing his or their hands. Perhaps from his classical education, he realized a deep truth. The philosopher Aristotle was once asked, "How has philosophy benefited you?" He replied, "I do without being ordered what others do out of fear of the law."[6] The law can supply the forms but not the function that these various ways of giving must serve. The latter comes from a mindful journey of discernment aimed at your family's well-being and enhancement.

Question:
What combination of form and function would be most likely to help your family members grow?

Notes

1. ABC News, "Exclusive: Buffett Kids React to Dad's Donation," *Good Morning America*, June 29, 2006, at http://abcnews.go.com/GMA/story?id=2133209&page=1.

2. By *trusts* we mean not only formal trust agreements but also other vehicles, such as corporations or limited partnerships, in which family members give their assets to someone else—a trustee, a board of directors, or a general partner—to steward those assets for their own or others' benefit. In addition, in civil law countries, where trusts are less used or nonexistent, we include such forms as the *waqf*, entail, usufruct, *fiduciario*, life estates, and the like. We speak specifically about trusts and trustees, but our conclusions hold for these other entities, too.

3. See James E. Hughes, *Family Wealth: Keeping It in the Family* (New York: Bloomberg Press, 2004), Chapter 21.

4. Roy Williams and Vic Preisser, *Preparing Heirs* (San Francisco, CA: Robert D. Reed, 2003), Chapter 2.

5. For examples of how trusts have positively impacted families' lives, see Hartley Goldstone's and Kathy Wiseman's innovative "Trustee-Beneficiary Positive Story Project" at www.navigatingthetrustscape.com.

6. See Diogenes Laertius, "Aristotle," in *Lives of Eminent Philosophers*, trans. R. D. Hicks (Cambridge, MA: Harvard University Press, 1972), p. 462, sec. 20.

THE WHAT AND WHY OF GIVING

Chapter 12

What Families Give

Gifts can take a million different shapes, from cash or securities to other items, such as homes or businesses, to such intangible but still powerful matters as values, rituals, and reputation. Our aim in this chapter is not to discuss these gifts in depth or to go into the legal complexities surrounding some of them. For those of you who have such technical knowledge, what we say here may serve to add a human element to the experience of giving these gifts. For others, our thoughts may start a path of thinking about gifts you have not considered yet. In any event, our goal is to share some stories and ideas and present some of the main questions for you to consider in your own journey of mindful giving. As always, we seek to understand not just the gifts but the development of human freedom and growth that their giving makes possible.

Homes

If you have lived in the same home for many years, you know its emotional power. The power only increases if you raised your children there, or if it is a vacation home where you and your family have spent many carefree days. This power explains why the gift of a family home can be one of the greatest meteors parents can send their children's way. A home almost always embodies spirit, especially if it is the home in which some of the recipients grew up. If you are considering such a gift, the question is not how to instill it with spirit but rather how to make the gift in such a way that the spirit works upon recipients positively.

The most obvious challenge to such a gift is that your family has likely multiplied over the years. How to divide one estate among, say, four adult children and their children? This matter of arithmetic becomes even more difficult when you throw finances into the mix. Homes are not cheap. The costs of maintaining them only increase each year. But financial wealth has a way of dividing and diminishing as each generation offers more mouths to feed. Increased costs and diminished assets are not a promising mix. The first consideration, then, is whether your children or grandchildren will be able to afford the home. As special as a home is, a gift that depletes your descendants is not much of a gift.

But arithmetic, finances, and demography—the quantitative matters—often pale next to the human challenge raised by giving a home. Different children or branches of the family will likely have different visions of how to use or not use the family home. Author George Howe Colt poignantly described these challenges with regard to his own family's summer home, nicknamed "the Big House," on Cape Cod: "I can hardly believe it even as I write these words—we are selling the Big House. Like many extended families throughout the Northeast whose rambling summer-houses were built in another, palmier era, we can no longer afford to keep up the place." Colt notes that the quantitative problem is an expression of a deeper, qualitative challenge: "*The financial issues are entwined with emotional issues far more formidable.* The house has come to mean something very different to each of the siblings in my father's generation who jointly inherited it after my grandmother's death in 1986. During two years of meetings whose veneer of civility could not wholly conceal the strong feelings that lay beneath, the family was unable to come to an agreement that would enable them to keep any part of the place." The result: "Four years ago, it was put up for sale."[1]

It is possible to surmount these financial and emotional challenges. Colt captures the steps that many families have taken to preserve estates over generations, even if their bank accounts do not keep up with demography: "Some families find ways to hang on to the ancestral estate. They convert boathouses and bathhouses into cottages for cousins. They lop off and sell chunks of land until their grand old summerhouse is, like a castle among peasant huts, surrounded by smaller homes and condominiums. They apply for conservation easements that require them to leave a certain portion of their property undeveloped in return for a tax reduction. They set up family trusts to pass vacation homes from generation to generation, appointing a trustee to administer the property, levying annual assessment to pay taxes and finance repairs." These strategies require work: "Such arrangements, in which the family becomes a kind of corporation and the house a commodity, seem contrary to the informal spirit of a summer place." Nonetheless, "they enable families to hold onto their homes."[2]

It is important to consider these challenges and possibilities before making the gift of a home. As Colt's story makes clear, the main challenge is the human one, related to freedom: How can you make sure that the recipients of your gift will feel free to work together to use the home in whatever ways they wish, perhaps years after you are gone?

Meeting that challenge starts with articulating the reasons you want to keep the home in the family. Only if you are clear can you productively engage future recipients. The next step is to invite your children or other recipients into the deliberation. Different children will likely have different views regarding the significance of a home.

Do not be surprised if for some children the possible gift of the family home brings back problematic memories or feelings.

For them, the spirit of the gift takes the form of ghosts. Others may feel strongly attached to a home but are hesitant to voice their attachment. For example, we once met a young woman who was in great distress because her father had announced that when he died, he wanted to see the family estate sold and the proceeds disbursed to his children. This young woman had grown up in the home. She wanted to live there after her father's death. But her father knew nothing of her desire. We helped the two of them meet and talk about the daughter' wishes, and as a result, the father amended his plans to allow her to retain the right to live in the home during her life, with suitable compensation to her siblings.

These conversations are not easy to have, especially if you are still living in your home. If you have lived there a long time, you probably hold strong views on how you want it to be maintained. (One mother we knew sold her home to her son, but then got upset when he changed the window treatments.) Still, try to include all the would-be recipients of the gift in the conversations, so that they can begin to communicate with you and each other about the use of the home. Some may eventually want to sell the home and pocket their share of the proceeds. Others may want to stay there but may not have the means to buy out their future partners. If some children do not want part of the home, you may wish to leave them other assets instead. Or you can structure the gift so as to give future owners a clear exit plan. Though it is not about making money, owning a home together is like running a business. People do best when they have a free choice to be part of the business or not.

A home is a complex gift. But with ample discussion and planning, it can provide a center for family life and activities for years to come. The key is to make sure that your family has the freedom to let the vision of the home grow and change with the family's vision of itself.

Business Interests

A share in a family owned or family controlled business is a gift unlike any other. Such a business is often a family's major source of wealth. If you own or control a family business, then other members of your family are likely relying on your wise choices for their financial well-being. What is more, if your family has a business, the business probably gives your family an important part of its very sense of identity and togetherness. The business may become the wellspring of the family's stories and the object of its dinner table and holiday conversations. It may feel like a family member—perhaps the most important member of all!

Not surprisingly, ownership of, control over, and enjoyment of business interests exert great power within business-owning families. Gifts of these interests must be made with great care.[3]

How can you do so? A good starting point is to distinguish, first in your mind and then in other family members' minds, between shares in the family owned business and other assets. A share of common stock is really a right, a right to enjoy a share in a company's future earnings. But a share of stock in a family owned company is something else altogether. It is a responsibility. You probably are among few owners of this stock. You exert great power over the direction of the company. Your decisions will affect the lives of your family members (perhaps especially older family members who rely on income from the business to live) and the lives of the business's executives and other employees.

Because ownership in a family business is such a big responsibility, many successful families treat it as something to be earned rather than given. You may believe that your children should enjoy the family's *financial* fortune by virtue of being born into the family. But you may also say that being born into a family is not reason enough to share in the ownership of a family *business*. You can set conditions for ownership: If your children are to own stock in the family business, they need to demonstrate their understanding of the business, their commitment to continue to learn, and their ability to care for the business and its resources, human and otherwise. As we have said before, every gift requires some preparation, on the part of recipients, for them to integrate the meteor successfully into their lives. Gifts of family business interests require a whole other level of preparation and integration. They really are only for the right recipients.

For these reasons, you may want to consider limiting the gift of business interests to family members who have worked their way to executive positions within the company. That does not mean that you must exclude other family members a share in the family's fortune. That would only provoke bad feelings and perhaps conflict. Instead, consider making provisions—through savings or insurance—to provide financial gifts to some members and business interests to others.

Exclusion from owning part of the business may still trouble some family members. (Consider the resentment felt in *The Godfather* by the son-in-law, Carlo, and the bumbling son, Fredo, both of whom were largely excluded from the family's business.) Family members who also serve as executives and who receive business interests may feel that they have already worked for this gift. These possibilities point to the need for you to reflect, mindfully, on what you really believe is right, make your decisions in a centered way, and then communicate those decisions openly and empathically with all affected family members and nonfamily executives.

If the gift of a family business is to be a freeing experience, then another consideration is also crucial. Business can be all-consuming. But successful families do not let involvement in the family business become a stand-in for membership in the family. In a family with a business, there is a natural tendency to equate membership in the business, either as an owner or executive, with membership in the family. But this equation will, over time, wear away the family's connectedness, because it represents a narrow vision of those connections. Only a limited number of family members can be effective owners and executives. If excluded from feeling truly part of the family (because they are not part of the business), the family members who are not owners or executives will likely lose interest in the business and their business-owning or business-managing relatives. This loss of interest lays the ground for future splits and conflict, which may eventually upset the business's success.

To guard against this possibility, first distinguish between membership in the family, the owners-group, and the company's managers (see Figure 12.1).

Then ask yourself, which of these circles plays the biggest role in our lives? Is being an executive what really counts? Are we leaders spending all our time focused on succession planning in the executive suite? If so, then your diagram may truthfully look more like Figure 12.2.

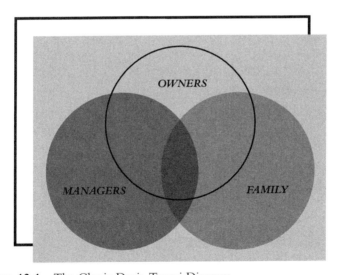

Figure 12.1   The Classic Davis-Taguri Diagram
SOURCE: John Davis and Renato Tagiuri, Harvard working paper, 1982, reprinted in *Family Business Review* 9, no. 2 (1996).

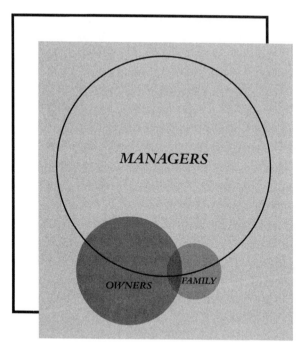

Figure 12.2 The Reality for Many Family Businesses

Or ask yourself, do we focus on who owns the shares and elects directors? Are we spending our time talking about buy-sell agreements and the education of future owners? If so, then perhaps your diagram should look like Figure 12.3.

These two variations on the three-circle model are the most common. It is not at all rare for either the *management* circle or the *ownership* circle to dwarf the other two. But in both cases, the family circle just gets smaller and smaller. If that is the case in your family, then your task is evident: to try to do what you can to grow that family circle. Ideally, the family circle should be larger than the other two, not smaller (see Figure 12.4).

By growing the family circle, you ensure that your family members have ways of connecting and spending time together

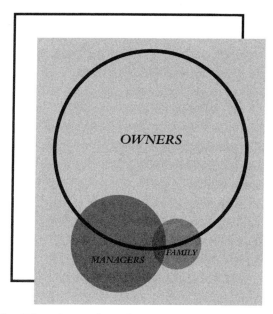

Figure 12.3 When Ownership Takes Over

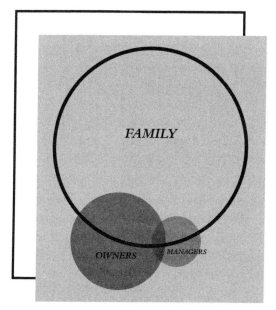

Figure 12.4 Giving Family Its Place

apart from business. You will also lay the foundation for communicating appropriate information about the business and its well-being broadly throughout the family, so that even those who are not in the business know how it is doing. By growing the family circle, you can create a sense of identity that honors the important place of the business without minimizing or excluding members who are not active within it.[4]

If you are contemplating gifts of business interests, one more consideration is crucial: discussing prenuptial arrangements with recipients of the gifts.[5] To recall Sigmund Freud's admonition once more, there is nothing harder to talk about than love, work, and money—and family business brings all three altogether. Dealing with these complexities requires a truly systemic approach. As we said in Chapter 5, prenups can be a destructive meteor. But there are compelling arguments for having prenuptial arrangements for members of a family for whom a business is important. The company is a family asset and ongoing enterprise that may have been in place for a number of generations, and many families want to see the business continue to grow for many more generations. A business family's financial future is interconnected in a way that is different from a family whose worth may consist of marketable securities that allow each member to manage his or her own financial affairs independently. Having a vital business requires an interdependence among family members that is best served without competing outside interests of non-blood relatives or possible divorce disagreements.

Helping a business thrive over several generations is one of the most rewarding tasks a family can undertake. It is also the gift that most obviously comes with a variety of strings and expectations attached. As a result, it takes careful consideration and communication. Taking those steps well is a gift to the business and to the family as a whole.

Values

In many discussions of estate planning or wealth management, you may hear references to value (singular), such as the value of an account, or a share or stock, or a trust. Very often you can also hear references to values (plural). You may have asked yourself, how can I make sure that my children or grandchildren inherit not just my money but also my values? It is one of the most pressing questions that parents face and that prompt them to take family giving seriously.

When considering that question, first reflect, for yourself, where it comes from. Sometimes behind that question is fear, the fear that the larger your children's bank accounts, the smaller they will become as human beings. More positively, most parents recognize that "man does not live by bread alone." Our values give direction and purpose to our material resources. If your children are to have large bank accounts, you likely want them to have solid values that give purpose to their wealth. As we have mentioned before, clearing your own lenses about your intentions is the place to begin.

If you are seeking to pass on your values, the natural next step is to ask yourself, what are my values? As part of this process, it may help to distinguish between your *actual* and your *aspirational* values. You can begin to identify your actual values by reviewing what your main activities have been over the past year or two. How have you spent your time? What have you sought to do? What have you avoided? Most importantly: Why? Distilling these answers down to single words will reveal the actual values that have been guiding your activities.[6]

You can do the same for your aspirational values: How would you like to spend the next year or two? What would your main activities be? Why? These answers will reveal your aspirational values, which may or may not be the same as your actual values.

Next, compare what you say to others—such as your children or grandchildren—about your values with what those values are.

What you say to others about values may map more closely to your aspirational rather than your actual values. In other words, like most of us, you may find it easier to talk the talk than to walk the walk. That is no reason to berate yourself. Instead, it is a good occasion to ask yourself how to bring your actual living into closer alignment with your words and your aspirations.

Once you are clear about your values, you can be more purposeful about the task of sharing those values with others. Think about the various things you may mean when you say that you want your children to inherit your values. It may be that you want to instill your values *in* your children. Such instillation implies helping your children develop good character, a process that takes many years and much habituation. It may be that you also want your children to develop their own values. That implies wanting your children to lead authentic lives, which requires a period of searching, questioning, and clarification of their own most important beliefs. The two processes can go hand-in-hand: good character provides the foundation from which one can freely pursue and develop sound values.

How can you help your children or grandchildren develop good character? We have already commented on how closely related family giving is to parenting generally. One of the things that we frequently tell families is that the key to being a good parent with wealth is to be a good parent simply. Doing so takes time, attention, patience, and humility.

Helping children develop their own values also takes time and patience. And it requires a healthy dose of communication. Respect for values, as a gift, means respecting your own and others' values. Your children and grandchildren may not share your beliefs. Communication makes it possible to respect each other as reasonable people while perhaps disagreeing about beliefs. It also makes it possible for you to see and trust the character of your children and grandchildren even if you question or even dislike their values.

Parents or grandparents sometimes take the step of saying that unless their descendants inherit their values they will not get their money. It is not an unreasonable proposal. After all, if you have worked hard to create wealth, why would you want to see it used in the service of values you question or abhor?

If you are contemplating making your financial gifts contingent on your descendants' values, be mindful of the distinction between values and character. There are many worthy values in the world. What is more, people often hold different values or beliefs at different points in their lives. Character is not as multitudinous or changeable. Good character has a relatively limited number of manifestations. Whatever someone's values, character will reveal itself. Ask yourself about a particular recipient: Am I reacting to her values? Or am I reacting to her character? If you dislike the values but you trust the character, then you probably do not have to worry about your financial gifts being misused. If the situation is reversed, then proceed more cautiously.

As a giver, it is always important to start your process of discernment with yourself. We all go through different stages in our lives. Your children or grandchildren may upset you with their focus on themselves, but such a focus is not unnatural in people in that first stage of life. They may be nowhere near the generative position that you find yourself in. Also, it is crucial to ask whether the interest in values is something you have felt lifelong or rather a relatively recent development. If the latter, where does it come from? From your character? From fear? From a desire to control? From a desire to judge? Or from a desire to enhance?

Finally, if you are a parent, you probably know that young people learn most from examples rather than words. The truth is that most of us do not always live our values. Have your children or grandchildren seen your values embodied in your actions? Or have they only heard about your values, expressed in your words? In the face of all these considerations, humility is a key virtue for family members seeking to make their values part of the spirit of their gifts.

Rituals

It may seem odd to think of family rituals as a form of gift. After all, we have emphasized throughout this book that true gifts free both the giver and the recipient. But people often think of rituals as constraining their freedom. Rituals come with traditional words, phrases, and actions. It is hard to change rituals. Are they just relics from times past meant to tie us down?

This attitude, in our view, comes from confusing rituals with their most visible manifestation: ceremonies. Ceremonies—such as weddings, baptisms, or funerals—usually are marked by traditional words and deeds. But these ceremonies truly mark the end of the ritual and the start of a new stage of life. They are not the rituals themselves. This distinction is an important one for understanding the role of rituals in promoting freedom and their status as a great gift.

Rituals have three main stages.[7] The first is a break with the everyday course of life. It usually involves some sense of realizing that one cannot go back to the old way and consequently a sense of mourning. The second stage involves the creation of a space apart from the rest of life in which new knowledge can be developed or new information is shared with the participants of the ritual. Third comes the reentry of the participants back into everyday life and the integration of what they have learned in that parallel space. This third stage is the one usually marked by ceremonies, which publicly indicate the start of the new stage of life.

Rituals may sometimes look silly, but they always serve a serious end. Here are some conspicuous examples:

Coming of age. Families often ritualize *the coming of age* of their members. That moment may involve moving from the kiddie table to sit with the grown-ups at Thanksgiving. Or it may involve learning about your trust from a trustee. Such rituals often involve the young person being taken away from his parents and being taught crucial information, including some of the group's secrets and important lessons about what it means to be an adult. It may involve spending time with others of the same age, such as at a next generation retreat. Confirmations and *bar* or *bat mitzvoth* are prominent examples of this type of ritual.

Creation of a new elder. As we described in Chapter 8, growing elders is key to growing families. A new elder's creation marks an extremely important point in the development of a family because it recognizes the willingness of the group as a whole to grant an individual the authority to mediate its disputes, to help enforce its rules of governance, and to preserve its stories. The evolution of an individual member to this status is also a major developmental step for that individual, since it is often an indication that she has finished her individual work and is now seen as ready to act for the group as whole.

Birth of a new member. All families celebrate *the birth of new members.* These rituals not only announce the individual's arrival but also offer the family a way of reaffirming the generations from which the child springs. More important still, this ritual gives all current family members a means to reaffirm the possibilities for their future.

The marrying in of a new member. Marriage is another important developmental step in the life of the individual entering the community and of the community itself. The rituals marking the entry of a new member celebrate the growth of the community and legitimize the new member's right to be a part of that community. Marriage is the most obvious such ritual, but a prior element may be the process of conversation about prenuptial arrangements.

Introduction of a new member. Families seeking to ensure that they are well-governed introduce into their family circle trustees, protectors, and advisors. Rituals to celebrate the arrival of such individuals represent an important celebration of their roles and a legitimization of their future authority and responsibility in family life and governance.

The death of a member. Deaths are ritually observed by all families. Rituals to help the individual members honor the life of the deceased not only assist the survivors in their individual grieving but also offer them a way to integrate the key events of the deceased's life into the stories that bind them together as a family.

In all these examples the point of the ritual is not to constrain members or limit their freedom but rather to lay the foundation for their future growth. If human beings grew like trees, in a steady, linear fashion, perhaps we would not need rituals. But our growth is discontinuous: We often break with past stages of life and jump to new ones. Rather than trees, we are more like lobsters and crabs, who have to crack and shed their old shells if they are to thrive. By acknowledging these psychic realities and providing a process for moving ahead, rituals create the conditions for truly human freedom. That is why developing, preserving, and handing on family rituals can be one of the greatest gifts in family life.

Reputation

Like ritual, reputation may seem an odd sort of gift. If you were born into a family of wealth, you were given the family name before you could ever hope to integrate that gift by choice. And anyway, "What's in a name?" as Juliet asked.

For a family, there may be quite a lot. According to sociologist George Marcus, a family name or reputation may, for a family of dynastic wealth, be its most enduring and powerful asset: "The value of a family name, on which a descendant can trade in various ways, is the most adaptive resource of a family/business formation, sustaining the external image and reviving itself in any later achievements of family descendants."[8] A 1970 Gallup study of the Rockefeller family came to a similar conclusion: "Here is a family whose vast wealth might be expected to generate envy, jealousy, and hatred; but instead it is seen predominantly by now as a dedication to public and humanitarian service for the good of mankind."

Growing, tending, and preserving a reputation can create an asset that may very well become the family's crown jewel in generations to come. Only one Rockefeller, David, made it onto the 2012 Forbes 400 list (at number 159), but the value of the name Rockefeller enriches all his family members.

How can you build your family's reputation as an asset? Though such activities as monitoring online uses of the family name and preparing public relations crisis communication plans are important, building true reputation goes beyond these tactical measures. Cultivating reputation (as distinct from publicity) involves being mindful of three main areas of work:

1. *Communication.* Giving the gift of reputation depends on good communication. To communicate well, families need to have a practice, such as a regular process of family meetings and thoughtful plans for communicating estate planning or other sensitive financial information.

2. *Education.* It is difficult to preserve and enhance a reputation if you do not know what it signifies. One important step is to educate younger family members or people new to the family in the family story. In addition, improper disclosures of family information (or misinformation about the family) can be averted by a plan of family wealth education, which gives younger or newer family members developmentally appropriate information about the family's affairs at agreed-upon points in their lives.

3. *Character development.* For families with significant wealth or business interests, preserving reputation often comes down to

developing character. No plan can control what every family member says or does. Living the family's reputation depends on character, habits, and choices. Developing character requires modeling by older family members and honest discussions of what the family's values are and how those values are played out in business or philanthropy.

This last point reveals how family character is something different than individual character. The word *character* comes from a Greek word meaning "stamp." Family character is the stamp the family makes on the world. Giving the gift of reputation means clarifying what that stamp is or should be, answering the question, What makes our family different or special?

How would you answer that question? Most people do so by reaching for distinctive stories about themselves and their ancestors. These stories often involve tales of struggle, journeys, defeats, and successes. Almost every family has its *Odyssey* and its *Iliad*, its saga of a long journey and a painful victory (or loss). These stories are an expression of the family's *lineage*.

Lineage does not just happen; it requires our efforts to keep it alive. These efforts raise the question of what it is that we should seek to preserve. Your answer to that question will shape the difference your family makes in the world. It will shape your family's character, or stamp, now and into the future.

Because of the power of lineage, we see its cultivation as the true core of the gift of reputation. Giving reputation is much more than monitoring the family's online profile or managing a public relations crisis. It is about defining, preserving, and redefining lineage.

How your family approaches this task means the difference between seeking to protect and then live off the family name—with the name becoming a sort of subsidy—and seeking to enhance the family's lineage and role in the world. This possibility of enhancement points to the connection between lineage and spirit. Ultimately, a family's lineage extends beyond itself—and certainly far beyond the intentions of any given family member, even the founder of the fortune. Individual family members will find inspiration and growth from spiritual sources outside the family, such as from religion or other spiritual traditions, and these spiritual inspirations will help define your family's lineage. In turn, your family will benefit the larger world, and that public benefit will further define your family's lineage. Every thriving family's true lineage stretches beyond family history into the history of humanity. True lineage never remains confined within a genealogical tree. In considering lineage, we come to the limits of family life. Family is important, but it is not everything. Families come to be and dissolve, but the spirit continues, before and after.

For these reasons, we believe that the gift of reputation or lineage addresses one of the core concerns that parents voice about giving wealth to their children: Will my gifts make my children feel entitled? The gift of lineage is an antidote to that ill.

Not long ago the word *entitled* meant simply that one had inherited a title of nobility. That title gave its holder a place within a social order, within a family, and most of all within a lineage, stretching back into the past and forward into the future.

The newer meaning of *entitlement* is, of course, quite different. Now an entitled person bears no distinguishing title, and yet he feels different from others. Far from having a place, he seems cut off from others and the social order. He does not give; he takes.

In its former usage, entitlement implied lineage. Its current use implies something very different. This newer entitlement is at odds with lineage. Both have a past, but the one embraces it while the other rejects it. Why? Because the former has a future, while the latter does not. The holder of a title of nobility knew that, at some point, he would pass that title to someone else. Today's entitled person lives only for himself. Far from being freer than old-time nobles, the newly entitled person looks sadly limited and small.

Lineage, then, is a key corrective to entitlement. A sense of lineage helps people avoid feeling cut off from the past and the future. It gives them a feeling of place and of worth within that place. Whether rich or poor, when we discover our lineage, we

discover our sense of being gifted. From that sense comes gratitude and the desire to pay forward the gifts we have received to
benefit others. If you give your descendants the gift of lineage,
you are not saddling them with constraining traditions or stories.
You are freeing them to receive and give gratefully. And you are
freeing yourself by knowing that you have mindfully prepared for
their resilience, growth, and freedom.

> **Question:**
> What is the most important thing you have to give?

Notes

1. George Howe Colt, *The Big House: A Century in the Life of an American Summer Home* (New York: Scribner, 2003), 13.

2. Colt, *The Big House*, 244.

3. For more on maintaining dynamic ownership in a family business, see James E. Hughes, *Family: The Compact among Generations* (New York: Bloomberg Press, 2007), Chapter 15.

4. Again, as Roy Williams and Vic Preisser found, it is the absence of such communication—rather than the failings of technical or quantitative planning—that dooms many business-owning families. See note 4 in Chapter 11.

5. We touched on this topic in Chapter 5, when discussing giving in the context of the spousal relationship. See pages 51–53.

6. There are many exercises that you can use to go through this process of discerning your values. The one we offer here is a simplification of the process embodied in Dr. Dennis Jaffe's Values Edge. See www.dennisjaffe.com.

7. See Arnold Van Gennep, *The Rites of Passage*, trans. Monica B. Vizedem and Gabrielle L. Caffee (Chicago: University of Chicago Press, 1960).

8. George E. Marcus with Peter Dobkin Hall, *Lives in Trust: The Fortunes of Dynastic Families in Late Twentieth Century America* (Boulder, CO: Westview Press, 1992), 42.

Chapter 13

The Why of Giving

We have discussed *the who* of family giving—recipients, givers, spouses, grandparents, trustees, and elders. We have reviewed some of *the how*, including the balance between control and freedom, fair and equal, separate and together, as well as outright giving, gift loans, and trusts. And we have touched on some of the most common gifts besides money or securities, including homes, business interests, values, rituals, and reputation. In all these discussions we have asked how gifts may enhance lives rather than merely subsidize individual lifestyles. We have repeatedly posed these questions as signposts for your own journey of discernment or mindful giving.

But we have not yet taken up another central question: Why? Why you decide to give (or not give) to this or that child or grandchild is something you must answer, based on your values, beliefs, and experiences, and based on the character and needs of the recipient. But why give to family members at all? As we shall see, answering the question of why brings us back full circle to answering the query with which we started: Can a family succeed over the long term without a spiritual component at its core?

Why *Not*

It may seem natural to want to give to family members, but the question of why you should follow through on that desire is a real one. After all, strong arguments have been made *against* doing so—on the basis of the claim that such giving undermines a family's spiritual life. This view expresses itself in one of two ways. The first is the argument that gifts to family members should be strictly limited. The second is the claim that gifts to family members should be avoided, perhaps altogether.

The first and more common view has been expressed well by famed investor and billionaire Warren Buffett, who said about his own family, "I want to give my kids just enough so that they would feel they could do anything, but not so much that they would feel like doing nothing."[1] Many other parents have adopted this mantra.

Industrialist Andrew Carnegie advocated the second point of view most famously and powerfully over a hundred years ago.[2] Carnegie held that "the most injudicious" use of surplus wealth is to give it to one's children.[3] Carnegie was also not a fan of making large bequests to charity upon death. Instead, he called on wealth holders to "administer" their fortunes during life "for the common good."[4] He inspired generations of philanthropists to do just that.

Why do Carnegie, Buffett, and many others thus argue against giving to family members? We have already raised some of their concerns. They fear that gifts will lead to entitlement. They see examples of gifts causing dependency. They have observed such giving inspire family conflict. Some also fear that family giving will lead to entrenched inequality and social unrest. It may be natural to want to share your wealth with your children and grandchildren, but, Carnegie replies, the "thoughtful man" will conclude, "I would as soon leave to my son a curse as the almighty dollar."[5]

In other words, these critics of family giving also want to foster enhancement rather than subsidies, growth rather than entropy. They conclude that such enhancement is more likely to come through philanthropic rather than family giving. In other words, these critics start from the same principles we have started from. We all want to enhance lives through a mindful process of discerning the best uses for material resources. In their way, these critics also respect the importance of the cycle of the gift. As Carnegie explained, society gave him security, bought his steel, and made him rich. He received that gift and then sought to give it back in turn. The same cycle of the gift that we have been talking about in the context of family helps explain why so many people find the call to give back through philanthropy so appealing.

That said, very few wealth holders pursue this plan of giving philanthropically rather than to family in the principled way that Carnegie did. Carnegie's vision of the cycle of the gift (grounded in society) is only one possible vision. A different view (grounded in family) is that we all receive good things from our parents, even if our parents are very poor, as were Carnegie's.[6] These good things—whether character, skills, knowledge, or material resources—help us, the recipients, do well in life, including perhaps grow wealthy. As our parents age and pass away, we cannot simply give back to them. Instead, most people feel a desire and obligation to give in turn to their own children, including sharing our dreams and some of the realization of those dreams, in the form of wealth. The stance for giving to family members and the stance against giving to family members each arises from a different version of the cycle of the gift.

The critique of family giving articulates real concerns. Still, even if our heads incline us to Carnegie's argument, our hearts move most parents and grandparents to leave more than a modest allowance to our descendants if we can. Also, the critics seem to assume that family giving cannot be done well. As the previous chapters have shown, we believe that mindfulness and resilience can help parents and children integrate wealth more positively into their lives and families. By sharing this mindfulness, we hope to help wealth holders align their heads with their hearts more completely than these critics' stern approach allows.

The Family Tree

This alignment comes from keeping the spirit and the cycle of the gift in mind. It comes from families' reflecting on themselves and their values. It comes from honestly seeking to understand recipients and to develop their resilience. It comes from engaging in a process of discernment about how gifts may enhance lives rather than subsidize status.

In other words, as we proposed in Chapter 1 after talking about Albert and Adele, family giving offers an opportunity to exercise human excellence. Pursued mindfully, it is hard work. Think of all those letters that George Peabody and his siblings, nieces, and nephews wrote back and forth to each other in the days before telephones and airplanes! It involves many different considerations. That is why more than two and a half millennia ago, Aristotle held that giving well is one of the most important virtues.[7] Giving well to family can exercise some of the best and highest qualities of the human soul. The cultivation of such virtue is, we believe, the ultimate answer to the question, why give to family members?

We have reviewed many considerations and practices that we believe are essential to the subject of giving. We want to close by emphasizing two practices that we see as crucial for making family giving succeed: humility and thankfulness. To convey their importance, we will share one more story, borrowed from the Roman philosopher Cicero.

In his beautiful essay "On Old Age," Cicero speaks of a young man who is traveling along a road. From the road he sees an old man planting a sapling in his yard. The young man thinks this strange, since he doubts that the old man will ever live to see the tree mature. So he calls out, "Old man, who are you planting that tree for?" The old fellow looks up and replies, "For the immortal gods, who wished that I not only receive these things from my ancestors but also that I give them to my descendants."[8]

We can learn a lot from this old man. He was first and foremost a recipient of good things from those who came before him. In turn, he sought to make a tangible gift: a young tree, planted by his own hands. His gift was for his children, grandchildren, and even great-grandchildren. He was thinking ahead, in an optimistic way. He had hope. Perhaps that is why he adds that he plants the tree first and foremost for the immortal gods. The gods do not need the shade. But they sanctify the cycle of the gift. They want us not just to take from those who came before but also to give to those who come after us. The old man seeks the gods' approval, in the hope that they will help bring his gift to fruition.[9]

This story reminds us that though a virtue, family giving need not be grandiose. The essence of family giving can be captured well and beautifully in something as simple and yet as profound as a tree. In fact, such giving happens all the time, when people pay for their children's schooling, or buy them bicycles, or give them a safe and stable home. As we have emphasized, all parenting is a form of family giving. And parenting embodies hope.

The story also emphasizes growth. Affluent families often focus on how much they have. Perhaps you can buy homes for all your adult children or pay for school for all your grandchildren. But in thinking about what is *buyable*, we easily lose sight of what is *desirable*. The real challenge facing families in giving is not to figure out the right structures or decide on the best procedures. The real challenge is to focus on function rather than form: to enhance rather than subsidize our lives with the same purposefulness as an old man planting a tree.

In this way, the story of the tree brings us back to language that Jay Hughes introduced in *Family Wealth*.[10] Successful families discern four types of capital—financial, social, human, and intellectual. If you have come this far in the journey, you likely recognize that your main concern is not caring for your financial capital. You can oversee competent advisors to do that. You also see that attending to social capital—togetherness, communication, and decision making—is necessary but not sufficient. For social capital relies on a deeper source: your family members' human and intellectual qualities. Your shared task is to discern how to foster these qualities, present and future.

To succeed, this endeavor requires humility. The old man has his hands in the dirt (the *humus*, from the same root, so to speak, as *humility*). Some people may argue that family giving lacks vision or impact. But there is something appealing in the humble desire to grow the family tree. Further, nothing is more humbling than parenting, and as a branch of parenting, family giving demands humility, too. As we have seen, gifts can wound those they are meant to help. The meteor of family giving can have a painful impact. And family relationships do tempt our vanity and pride, which, when frustrated, easily turn into anger or resentment. All of us make mistakes in our parenting and our family giving. The key is not to abandon the attempt but to pursue it with humility and hopefulness. Sometimes, one of the most lasting and meaningful gifts we can give to our children and to ourselves is the gift of forgiveness.

Giving Thanks

Clearly, giving well to family members requires discernment, and discernment begins with a reflective attitude.[11] Such reflection brings us face to face with how much is given in life—how much we have received, do receive, and will receive. If you think about the cycle of the gift as a cycle of individual development, you can recognize that you begin life with what is given. You begin life as a recipient and you end life as a recipient once more. Again, giving well rests upon receiving well.[12]

Thankfulness is at the heart of this task of receiving well. Receiving well begins with acknowledging *that* you are a recipient and *what* you have received. Giving thanks completes this acknowledgement. Giving thanks goes beyond saying a few words or sending a note, though such expressions are important. After all, we can give thanks even when we are not with—or do not even know—those who have benefited us. How is that? Because giving thanks means taking what you have received to heart. It means acknowledging—most fundamentally to yourself—that you recognize the spirit of the gift and that you have integrated it into yourself. In the deepest sense, being thankful is one with being mindful.[13]

This is the answer to our initial question about the importance of spirit to family flourishing: giving and receiving materialize the spirit in our families' lives. And that is what our journey has truly been about: the enhancement of life through spirit. These final reflections on humility and hopefulness, thanks and mindfulness bring us to the boundaries of family giving and hence locate family giving within the context of a larger life. The many gifts we have received, and our thankfulness for them, point us toward sources and a world that extends far beyond our families. Being humbly thankful for and mindful of that larger world, in turn, allow us to give our families what they need to flourish. Families do not invent the spirit of the gift; the spirit of the gift makes our families what they are. True discernment about the goals and limits of family giving highlight the excellence at work in it and so encourage us to take it all the more seriously.

Questions:
As you look back, what are you most grateful for?
As you look forward, how will you give back?

Notes

1. For a recent example, see Buffett's interview with Charlie Rose on June 26, 2006. Late in life, however, Buffett seems to be having second thoughts. For example, in 2011 he named his son Howard, an agronomist, his successor as chairman of investment company Berkshire Hathaway. Likewise, alongside an enormous gift to the Gates Foundation in 2006, Buffett gave each of his children $1 billion in philanthropic funds, a gift that none of them requested and that he did not discuss with them beforehand. For this last point, see Sarah Hampson, "Peter Buffett's Rich Life Doesn't Come from Family Wealth," *Globe and Mail*, November 1, 2011. As this book went to press, Buffett gave his children's foundations another few billion dollars—tellingly, on his own birthday, not on theirs.

2. Carnegie laid out his views in a series of articles that he then collected into a single volume: *The Gospel of Wealth and Other Timely Essays* (New York: The Century Co., 1900).

3. Carnegie, *Gospel of Wealth*, 9.

4. Ibid., 12.

5. Carnegie, *Gospel of Wealth*, 10.

6. Carnegie vividly recalls the sacrifices his parents made for him: "In after life, if you can look back as I do and wonder at the complete surrender of their own desires which parents make for the good of their children, you must reverence their memories with feelings akin to worship" (*Gospel of Wealth*, viii). Likewise, while he sentimentalizes poverty, he sees the neglect of parenting as the true loss wealthy families suffer: "As a rule, there is more genuine satisfaction, a truer life, and more obtained from life in the humble cottages of the poor than in the palaces of the rich. I always pity the sons and daughters of rich men, who are attended by servants, and have governesses at a later age, but am glad to remember that they do not know what they have missed" (*Gospel of Wealth*, xii).

7. See Aristotle, *Nicomachean Ethics*, Book 4, Chapter 1. For a translation, see Joe Sachs, trans. (Newburyport, MA: Focus Press, 2002).

8. "Dis immortalibus, qui me non accipere modo haec a maioribus voluerunt, sed etiam posteris prodere." For a translation of the full context, see Michael Pakaluk, "Cicero: On Friendship," in *Other Selves: Philosophers on Friendship* (Indianapolis, IN: Hackett Press, 1991). The translation used here is our own. In that translation, "give ... to" could also be rendered as "give them for" or "give them on behalf of." James E. Hughes

uses a similar story in *Family Wealth: Keeping It in the Family* (New York: Bloomberg Press, 2004), 12–13: The 19th century French Marshal Lyautey asked his gardener why his garden had no copper beech tree. The gardener replied that it takes such a tree 150 years to mature. The marshal responded, "Well then plant it this afternoon. We have no time to lose!" This story was retold by President John F. Kennedy in several speeches during his presidency to buttress his conclusion, "We must think and act not only for the moment but for our time." See, e.g., Kennedy's "Address at University of California Berkeley," March 23, 1962, and "Speech at Yale University," June 11, 1962.

9. The story of the old man makes explicit what was implicit in our dialogue with the family with the pot, a dialogue that resulted in the promise, "I will help you in your own journey of happiness, and I hope that you will help me in mine." See Chapter 10.

10. Hughes, *Family Wealth*, 16–19.

11. Since our living precedes our reflecting, our reflections start with our memory. The word *memory* comes from the Latin *memor*, which itself derives from *mens*, which means "mind." Memory, too, presents itself as given. We do not simply make our memories. They appear to us as mysterious fragments from mysterious sources—and are sometimes cherished all the more for their mystery. Memory is the initial form of mindfulness. In this regard, consider the words of the poet, William Carlos Williams: "Memory is a kind / of accomplishment / a sort of renewal / even an initiation. . . ." (in *Paterson*, Book 2, Part 3, page 1). See *Paterson*, revised edition, Christopher MacGowen, ed. (New York: New Directions, 1995).

12. Recall page 94.

13. For more on the meaning of *thanks*, the philosopher Martin Heidegger observes that the Old English words for *think* and for *thank* are closely related. A *thanc* (which survives in the plural *thanks*) was a thought, a grateful thought. The grateful thought both gives—the verbal expression, "Thank you!"—and takes: It takes what has been given to heart. More precisely, it takes to heart the meaning or spirit of what it has received. See Martin Heidegger, *What Is Called Thinking?* trans. J. Glenn Gray (New York: Harper & Row, 1968), 139–143.

Readers are reminded that they may find a regularly updated bibliography of readings related to giving and family wealth at www.thecycleofthegift.com.

About the Authors

James E. Hughes Jr., Esq.

A retired attorney and resident of Aspen, Colorado, Jay is the author of *Family Wealth: Keeping It in the Family*, *Family: The Compact Among Generations*, and numerous articles on family governance and wealth preservation as well as a series of "Reflections" that can be found on the Articles section of his website, jamesehughes.com.

Jay is the founder of a law partnership in New York City and has spoken frequently at numerous international and domestic symposia on the avoidance of the shirtsleeves-to-shirtsleeves proverb and the growth of families' human, intellectual, social, and financial capitals toward their families' flourishing.

Jay is a member of various philanthropic boards and a member of the editorial boards of various professional journals. He is a graduate of the Far Brook School, which teaches through the arts; The Pingry School, Princeton University; and The Columbia School of Law.

Dr. Susan E. Massenzio

Susan is a psychologist who sees wisdom as core to counsel. She is a founding associate of Wise Counsel Research Associates, a think tank and consultancy.

Susan has extensive experience consulting to senior executives, leadership teams of Fortune 500 companies, and heads of family businesses. She helps firms develop high potential executives, plan leadership succession, and integrate key leaders into new roles. She helps family leaders make a positive impact through enhanced communication, decision making, cultivation of the next generation, and philanthropy.

Susan served for many years as the senior psychologist for John Hancock Financial Services, a senior vice president at Wells Fargo, and professor and program director at Northeastern University.

Susan is a member of the Collaboration for Family Flourishing. She holds a PhD in psychology from Northwestern University and a BA in sociology and education from Simmons College.

In addition to her writing and speaking, Susan consults with select executives and heads of family enterprises around leadership, organizational development, and individual and family flourishing. If you would like to discuss an initial consultation, please contact Susan at susan@wisecounselresearch.com.

Dr. Keith Whitaker

Keith is an educator and founding associate of Wise Counsel Research Associates, a think tank and consultancy. His early introduction to the tradition of liberal education began his fascination with the spirit of the gift.

Keith has many years' experience consulting with advisors to and leaders of enterprising families. He helps families plan succession, develop next-generation talent, and communicate around estate planning. With a background in education and philanthropy, he enables family leaders to better understand their values and goals as well as to have a positive impact on the world around them.

Keith served as a managing director at Wells Fargo, where he founded the innovative Family Dynamics Practice. He has also served as a researcher at the Center on Wealth and Philanthropy, a private trustee, a director of a private foundation, and a philosophy professor at Boston College.

Keith's writings and commentary have appeared in the *Wall Street Journal*, the *New York Times*, the *Financial Times*, and *Philanthropy Magazine*. His *Wealth and the Will of God* (co-authored with Dr. Paul Schervish) appeared in 2010 from Indiana University Press.

Keith is a member of the Boston Estate Planning Council and a founding member of the Collaboration for Family Flourishing. He holds a PhD in social thought from the University of Chicago and a BA and MA in classics and philosophy from Boston University.

Keith speaks regularly about the themes of *The Cycle of the Gift* with families, membership organizations, and trade groups. If you would like to discuss a speaking engagement or initial consultation, please contact Keith at keith@wisecounselresearch.com.

Readers are reminded that they can find a regularly updated bibliography of readings related to giving and family wealth at www.thecycleofthegift.com.

Index

Acknowledgment, of financial
relationship, 54
Actual values, 131–132
Adolescence stage, goal of, 34
Adulthood stage, goal of, 34
Age
coming of, ritualizing the,
134–135
experience and, 83
reflecting on, 32
Angus, Patricia, 72
Annual exclusion gifts, 2, 3, 9, 90
Aspirational values, 131–132
Aspirations, gifts and, 19
Asset, family reputation as, 137
Autonomy *vs.* shame
and doubt, 33

Balancing act, 98–99
Beneficiaries
effects of trusts on, 111
trustee relationship with, 68, 69–73

Blended families, sharing wealth
and, 50–51
Buffett, Warren, 22, 31,
110, 142
Business interests, gift of,
125–130

Carnegie, Andrew,
91, 142, 143
Challenge (rather than threat),
43– 44
Character
development of, reputation
and, 137–138
manifestations of, 133
Charitable lead trust
(CLT), 100
Charitable remainder trust
(CRT), 100
Choice, of trustee, 67–68
Clearing your lenses,
19, 25–26, 29

CLT. *See* Charitable lead
    trust (CLT)
Cognitive-behavioral triangle
    approach, 80
Collier, Charles, 49
Colt, George Howe, 122, 123
Commitment (rather than
    alienation), 43– 44
Communication
  gift of reputation and, 137
  gifts and, 9–10
  with parents about giving, 60
  recipient's resilience and, 44–45
Community, 43– 44
Company's managers, 127
Control, 43– 44, 87–95
Conversation
  with gift recipients,
    Peabody and, 92
  between givers and recipients,
    39–40, 45, 91
  between grandparents and
    grandchildren's parents,
    58–59, 60
  with spouse regarding
    gifts, 47, 48
Core values, sharing, 12
CRT. *See* Charitable
    remainder trust (CRT)

Davis, John, 127
Davis-Taguri diagram, 127
Deaths, rituals and, 136
Despair, integrity *vs.,* 34
Developmental stages,
    giving and, 33–36
Disbursements, 114
Discernment process, 80–81,
    88–89, 115, 133, 146
Distinction, elders and sense of, 82

Divine Comedy (Dante), 83
Donor-advised fund, 62
Dreams
  givers and sharing, 19–20
  stewarding givers', 40–41
  The Yin-Yang Dilemma, 41
Dynasty trust. *See* Perpetual trust

Eastern nations, gifts and, 8
Elders
  growing, 79–81
  intergenerational dynamics,
    78–79
  new, rituals and creation of, 135
  work of, 81–84
Empathy, 29, 44
Enhancement, gifts and,
    9, 10–11, 143
Entitlement, 138
Entropy, 10, 11, 13, 143
Erikson, Erik, 32, 33, 34
Estate planning, 88–89, 100
Estate tax, 2
Expectations, gifts and, 19–20

Fairness *vs.* equality, 98
Fair *vs.* equal treatment, 98
Family
  blended, sharing wealth and,
    50–51
  flourishing, enhancing, 5, 102–104
  future growth of,
    focus on, 102, 103
  members of, 127, 135–136
  name of, 136–137
  reputation as gift, 137–140
  rituals and new member
    celebration, 135
Family bank, 108, 113–115
Family businesses, reality for, 128

Family character, 138
Family foundation, 100, 101
Family giving
    as an opportunity, 4–6
    challenges in task of, 100–102
    grandparent's checks and, 2–4
Family home, gift of, 121–124
Family limited partnership
    (FLP), 100
Family owned business, gift of,
    125–130
Family's core work,
    giving and, 5–6
Family tree, 144–146
Family trust, 100, 112
Feelings, gifts and, 8
Fiscal unequals,
    partnership of, 55–56
FLP. See Family limited
    partnership (FLP)
Form vs. function, 115–116
Foundation
    family, 100, 101
    private, 62
Four C's, 43–44
Franklin, Benjamin, 31
Freedom
    control vs., 87–95
    gifts and, 87–88, 91, 92
Freud, Sigmund, 129
Function, form vs., 115–116
Funds
    donor-advised, 62
    grandparent-grandchild
        philanthropic fund, 64–65
    philanthropic, 62, 63
Fusion, 10

Generation skipping tax, 2
Generativity vs. stagnation, 34

Gift(s). See also Business interests;
        Elders; Receiving gifts;
        Recipients of gifts
    annual exclusion, 2, 3, 9, 90
    benefit of, 88–89
    consequences for recipients, 31
    of family home, 121–124
    family rituals as, 134–136
    free, myth of, 87–88
    loans, 108, 109–110
    as meteor, xxix, 4, 29
    of money or property, 5
    outright, 108–109
    reputation as, 136–140
    spirit of, 7–13, 20, 26
Gift tax, 2
Givers
    discernment and, 133
    preparing ourselves as, 18–20
    recipients of gifts and, 17–18, 26
    views on using gifts, 88
    wealth and, 18
Giving. See also Family giving
    of accounts, 90–92
    arguments against, 142–144
    balancing control and freedom, 88
    elders and, 77–84
    grandparents and, 58–64
    guilt, 24–26
    letting go and, 94
    mindful, 42, 45
    psychological stages of, 32–36
    three-step process, 48–49
    wise, 17–27
    work ethic and, 36–39
Giving thanks, 146–147
Goals
    of adolescence and adulthood
        stages, 34
    of trustees, 67

Golden Rule, 55
Grandchildren, grandparent's
    connection with, 58
Grandparent-grandchild
    philanthropic fund, 64–65
Grandparents
    checks, 2–4
    connection with
        grandchildren, 58
    involving parents with
        giving, 58–64
    philanthropy and, 61–65
Grant committee, 62, 63
Grantor's remorse, 24–26
Grantor (trust creator), 68, 111
Grant-request process, 63–64
Guilt giving, 24–26

Happiness, enjoying, 103–105
Harvard working paper, 1982
    (Davis and Taguri), 127
Horizontal relationships, 55
Hughes, Jay, 72
Humility, 146

Identity vs. role confusion, 34
Immediacy, outright gifts and,
    108–109
Immigrants, in the land
    of wealth, 30–31
Individual development,
    cycle of gift and, 13
Individual trustees, 69
Industry vs. inferiority, 33–34
Inferiority, industry vs.,
    33–34
Initiative vs. guilt, 33
Institutional trustees, 69
Integration, gifts and, 29–30
Integrity vs. despair, 34

Intergenerational
    dynamics, 78–79
Intimacy vs. isolation, 34
Investment
    bad, 30–32
    in the future of children, 50
    recipients of gifts and,
        44–45
Isolation, intimacy vs., 34

Jobs, Steve, 31
Joy and fulfillment, cultivating,
    102, 103, 104

"Know thyself," 18–20
Koch, Charles, 22
Koch, David, 22

Life, stages of, 35–36
Lineage, sense, 103, 138–140

Maimonides, on levels of giving,
    xxx–xxxii
Marcus, George, 136
Marriage, rituals and, 135
Melville, Herman, 22
Mentor, trustee as, 73
Meteors
    of family giving, 146
    gifts as, 4, 29
    prenup arrangements and, 52
    resilience and, 41–44
Mindful giving, 42, 45
Money, gift of, 5, 21–22

Native Americans (Northwest),
    inheritance and, 8
Natives, in the land of wealth,
    30–31
"Nothing too much," 26–27

Oracle, Delphic, 20, 26
Outright gifts, 108–109
Owners-group, 127

Parenting, family giving
    and, 5–6
Parents
    focusing on children, 49
    prenup arrangements and,
        51–54
    resources and children's
        dreams, 45
Patience, elders and, 81
Peabody, George, 90–91
Perpetual trust, 111, 112–113
Philanthropic fund, 62, 63
Philanthropy, grandparents and,
    61–65
Piver, Susan, 54
Poor Richard (Franklin), 31
Power of spirit, in family giving,
    7–13
Preisser, Vic, 112
Prenuptial arrangements, 51–54
Private foundation, 62
Property, gift of, 5
Public charities, 62
Purpose, gift and, 27

Qualitative gift, 22
Quantity of money,
    giving and, 21–24

Receiving gifts
    letting go and, 94
    in stages of life, 34–36
Recipients of gifts
    consequences for, 31
    givers and sharing dreams
        with, 19–20

giving and understanding of,
    17–18, 26
investing in, 44–45
preparation and resilience of,
    42–43
Reputation, as gift, 136–140
Resilience, meteors
    and, 41–44
Rituals, family
    elders and, 83
    as gift, 134–136
Rockefeller, David, 137
Rockefeller, John D., 91
Rule against Perpetuities, 111

Self-efficacy, 43
Self-knowledge, 18–20
Senior generation, 78–79
Separation vs. togetherness,
    99, 101–102
Shame and doubt,
    autonomy vs., 33
Silence, family giving and, 4, 6
Social cycle of gift, 13
Social element, gifts and, 8
Spouses
    dealing with blended
        family, 50–51
    engaging with
        conversation, 47
    partnership of fiscal
        unequals, 54–55
    prenuptial arrangements
        and, 51–54
    sharing vision, 48–49
Subsidies, gifts as, 9, 10, 11
Successors, trustees and, 68

Taguri, Renato, 127
Temperament, reflecting on, 32

Templeton, Sir John, 79
Thankfulness, 146–147
Thoughtful givers, xxx, 82
Transfers, 9, 10
Transfer taxes.
    See Estate tax; Generation
    skipping tax; Gift tax
Transformation, gifts and, 9
Trust, 62
    Charitable lead trust, 100
    Charitable remainder
        trust, 100
    family, 100, 112
    gifts in, 108
    protectors of, 68
    reason for, 110–113
    vs. mistrust, 33
Trust creator (grantor), 68
Trust document
        (trust agreement), 68
Trustee(s)
    choice of, 67–68
    definition of, 68
    as mentor, 73
    regenerative role of, 74–75
    as regent, 72–73

relationship with beneficiary,
    69–73
type of, 69

Understanding, 17–18,
    26, 29
University of California–
    Berkeley's Greater Good
    Project, 5, 6
Unreflective giving, xxx

Values
    core, sharing, 12
    family, elders and, 83–84
    inheritance of, 131–133
Vanderbilt, Cornelius, 91
Vertical relationships, 55

Wealth
    givers and, 18, 19
    transfer of, 22–23
Wealth education,
        reputation and, 137
Williams, Roy, 112
Work ethic, giving and,
    36–39